BACK STREET KID

Growing up in Royal Leamington Spa

by

Valerie J Nunan

This book is dedicated to Dr Denise Hrouda
in appreciation of her willingness to look
beyond the date on my birth certificate when
deciding on my treatment.

Thank you, Doctor

My thanks also to all those staff at both
Warwick and Stratford Hospitals, who have
in any way contributed to my care.

6

Contents

1	In the Beginning	12
2	Bicycles, Bread and Witches	18
3	Number Twenty Park Street	26
4	How to Release a Head Stuck in Railings	39
5	An Aromatic Place	52
6	Cream Skirts and Coal Dust	60
7	Shopping with Mom	67
8	Books	82
9	The Gardens	92
10	Playtime	102
11	Cars, Bicycles and Shanks' Pony	111
12	Christmas	117
13	Granny Moore	126
14	The Dentist's Chair	134
15	St Peter's Church	147
16	Leamington Girl's College	155
17	Moving House	169
18	Happy Days	181
19	The End of Childhood	193

Appendix 1	My Paternal Grandparents	200
Appendix 2	Albert & Charles Cleaver	204
Appendix 3	Do not criticise your neighbour until you have walked a mile in his moccasins	207

Copyright © 2023 Valerie J Nunan

Introduction

Born in a Leamington backstreet in the summer of 1943, my childhood was very different to that lived by most children today. It was a time when the world was at war; a time when our island nation was short of food and rationing was introduced to make sure that everyone had a fair share. Many homes were still without electricity, and lavatories, sometimes shared with one's neighbours, were frequently to be found outside, at the end of the yard.

Few homes could boast a telephone, whilst television, still in its infancy, was usually to be found only in the homes of the better off. There were few cars on the road and even the purchase of a new bicycle might make a man the envy of his friends, who would gather round to examine it in much the same way that people might gather round a Porsche or a Ferrari today. Children walked to school; dads cycled to work and, in a time when there were few nurseries or labour-saving devices available, mums stayed home to care for the children and attend to the household chores. Supermarkets did not exist and shopping could be a lengthy business as it meant visiting any number of small shops and, at each one, waiting in a queue to be served.

Looking back, it is difficult to believe that so many of the things we take for granted today either did not exist, or were just in their infancy at the midpoint of the twentieth century; polio vaccinations, automatic washing machines, mobile phones, double glazing, microwaves... even the humble Sellotape, although invented in the 1930's, did not go into production properly until after the end of WW2.

The NHS was not formed until July 5th 1948, ensuring free health care for all. Although there were health services available before this, these were provided by a variety of different organisations; there seemed to be little joined-up thinking between them and most people had to pay. Lloyd George's National Insurance Act 1911, for instance, whilst providing free GP care for working-class men, did not cover their wives and children, or the middle classes. There were, in any case, few diagnostic tools, medications or treatments available.

Scans and keyhole surgery are both taken for granted today and yet they have only been introduced relatively recently, with the first scan in the world taking place at the Atkinson Morley Hospital in Wimbledon on October 1st 1971. Following this breakthrough, other hospitals gradually began to acquire scanning machines too, many of them paid for by the fund-raising activities of local communities.

The first keyhole surgery to be performed on a human being, actually took place as far back as 1910, but it was not until the latter part of the twentieth century that technology became sufficiently advanced to allow for it to become normal everyday practice.

Today, it is almost impossible to live without computers, so-much-so that my youngest son, born in January 1986 and having grown up with the machines, was astounded to learn that one of the first home computers, the ZX81, only came onto the market as recently as that year (1981). Small, simple and affordable, it had 1K as standard and was far removed from the computers we use today; nevertheless, it was an instant success, eventually selling one and a half million machines. A few years later, in 1989, Tim Berners Lee invented the World Wide Web and the whole world changed.

This book takes a step back in time to take a look at a world which was simpler and far less complicated than the one we inhabit today. Although I refer to it as a memoir, it is actually a mix of personal anecdotes, together with some social and local history. I hope you will find it interesting and that for some of you at least, it will provide a nostalgic trip down Memory Lane.

Chapter One
In the Beginning

"Went orf 'ome t'ave 'er breakfast, she did" Mom would frequently recount of Old Granny Cotton in a voice that was always loaded with shocked disbelief, "but she 'adn't got t' the top of ower street when me waters broke an' you cem with 'em. Yer dad 'ad t' go after 'er an' fetch 'er back". Thus, it was that I made my entrance into the world on a July morning back in the summer of 1943.

"You were tongue-tied", the parents would often tell me over the years and there have, indeed, been many occasions when shyness has stilled my tongue and rendered me speechless, but what they really meant was that I was born with ankyloglossia. More commonly known as tongue tie; this is a congenital condition in which the piece of skin anchoring the tongue to the floor of the mouth, is too short, thus 'tying' the tongue and restricting the movement of that all-important muscle.

Today, opinion seems to be divided on whether or not there should be early intervention and a wait and see approach is often adopted; however, at the time I was born, the condition was thought to affect a baby's ability to suck, or to cause speech problems in the growing child. That being so, the old village midwife did what she had always done when faced with this problem ... and simply set about remedying the situation herself with the aid of a very sharp pair of scissors!

Although no doubt distressing for Mom to witness, it must have been a great relief for my parents to find the problem rectified so easily; however, as I grew older and a great deal more voluble, there were many times when an exasperated Dad would be driven to declare, "Cuttin' yewer tongue were the wust days' work Old Granny Cott'n ever did; yer 'aven't stopped bloody yappin' since."

Until The 1902 Midwives Act, there was little formal training for midwives and women giving birth might simply be assisted by another female family member or perhaps a friend or a neighbour. The cost of employing a trained midwife prior to the formation of the NHS was set at 1s 6p, and extra if the help of a doctor was required. The first baby to be born free of charge on the NHS arrived at one minute after midnight on July 5th 1948. Had she arrived one minute earlier, then the parents would have had to pay the charge.

My mother's first baby had weighed in at a whopping 10lbs 6oz, a big baby by any standards and Mom was but a tiny wee slip of a woman. It soon became clear that she would require more help than Granny Cotton could give if she was ever to deliver the child and so the doctor was sent for and chloroform administered... When she came round again it was to discover that in addition to being the mother of a bonny baby girl, she had also become temporary custodian of the doctor's very own set of gold-plated suture clips. The baby was given the names Maureen Ambrose, the latter chosen by our grandfather, James Moore, who, having suggested this rather exotic name for his new granddaughter, then took to calling her by the rather less exotic sobriquet, 'ambone!

One Sunday morning soon after she was born, and with Mom still recovering from the birth, Dad took the baby visiting. Proudly he wheeled his first born in the direction of his home village of Cubbington, just a short distance away, there to be cooed over and cuddled by his admiring family, whilst he himself enjoyed a welcome cup of tea and caught up on the village news. The morning passed quickly and all too soon it was time to take his leave and begin the walk home to the house on The Holt, that he and Mom shared with her parents and younger brother.

It was hot and by the time he reached the main road and its popular watering hole, The Rugby Tavern, he was gasping for a drink. 'Surely it won't hurt to have just one pint.' he told himself, as he parked the pram and went inside. A short while later, feeling much refreshed, he continued on his way, but not until he arrived home again and Mom enquired about the baby's whereabouts, did he realise why his walk home had been dogged by the uncomfortable feeling that he had forgotten something!

The baby had grown into a healthy five-year-old on the day that she accompanied our mother down into the cellar to help put pennies in the gas meter. Pregnant with her second child, Mom picked her way carefully down the unlit flight of steps, holding firmly onto her daughter's small hand. Step by cautious step they descended towards the faint gleam of light illuminating the bottom. And then suddenly - disaster! In an unexpected fit of childish exuberance, Rene (Maureen) jumped down one step ahead of Mum, pulling her off-balance and sending her crashing down the remaining steps to the cellar floor below. The following day, on June 7th 1938, my mother went through the deeply distressing experience of giving birth to a stillborn son.

Moving forward to the night of November 14th 1940, my terrified mother could be found huddled beneath the kitchen table, tightly clutching her four-month-old daughter in her arms, as wave after wave of German Luftwaffe planes passed overhead, en route to bomb the medieval heart out of the City of Coventry. One pilot released his bombs too soon and a whole stick of six fell across Leamington's town centre, the first demolishing a house in York Road and killing the gentlemen within, and the last landing in the east side of Regent Street and no distance at all from my parents' Park Street home.

Apparently, this was not my mother's only encounter with the German Air Force, for she would often tell how she had been walking Rene home from school one lunchtime when a German plane hove into view and, according to Mom, "Flew the 'ole length of Warwick Street, 'e did, shootin' at everybody; we 'ad t' dive into Clarkes' shop an' tek cover there."

In spite of these experiences, my parents seemed not to have borne any animosity towards individual Germans and they later befriended a young prisoner-of-war named Werner Faulkner. I have no recollection of the young man at all but I clearly remember the wooden push-along ducks that he made for my sister and me. Cream coloured and daubed with splashes of red and green paint, they had long handles, wheels, and wings that flapped up and down as they were pushed along. My parents received one letter from Werner after he was transferred to a camp in Scotland - perhaps in preparation for his repatriation to Germany after the war ended - but after that, all contact seemed to have ceased.

Now it was January 1951 and Mom was waking us rather earlier than usual; me, curled up in the cot that had been my night-time home since the day I was born; and Pat, my elder sister, slumbering gently in the centre of the big double bed she shared with Mom and Dad. We were to go downstairs quietly and get ourselves dressed by the fire; we were told. "And DON'T touch the bundle on the chair" she warned. The tone of her voice was sufficient to have us instantly obeying and without even the tiniest murmur of dissent, we climbed out of our cosy sleeping places and, shivering in the cold early morning air, made our reluctant way down the narrow staircase.

The bundle we had been warned not to touch turned out to be a hand-knitted blanket worked in a pattern of broad red and cream stripes. It was resting on the seat of an armchair, pushed close up against the back, and it was very apparent that there was something quite bulky wrapped within its folds. "Don't touch", Mom had said -

which is just about as good an invitation to touch as a child can get. Glancing behind to check that she hadn't followed us, we quietly crept over to the chair and gently lifted a corner of the blanket. I don't know what it was that we expected to see ... but it was certainly not the tiny baby sleeping peacefully within, completely oblivious of the two astonished young girls staring down at it.

We shared the house with my father's nephew and his family, and so it was that a short time later, now back upstairs again, we found ourselves seated at the table in their living room, obediently eating the breakfast that 'Aunt' Marge placed before us. After a while, we heard men's voices coming from down below, followed by the sound of heavy footsteps mounting the uncarpeted stairs. Upon hearing them, Marge left the room, firmly shutting the door behind her. A short time later it opened again revealing two uniformed ambulance men carrying between them a canvas sling in which lay our mother, looking pale-faced and frightened. Catching no more than a glimpse before the little group moved out of view, we were unaware then that some time would pass before we would see our mother again.

Chapter Two
Bicycles, Bread and Witches

The way the seven-year-old me saw it, there were two kinds of bikes - those with two wheels and those with three. Back home I had one of the latter, passed down through my two sisters. Somewhat battered and bruised by the time it reached me, it nevertheless served its purpose and I had spent many enjoyable hours speeding down the hill, often with a small playmate standing on the back looking for all the world like a charioteer going into battle, so when Uncle Tom enquired one day if I could ride a bike, I replied with all innocence that I could. This seemed to satisfy him and no more was said until the morning of my eighth birthday when he and Auntie took me out to the yard and showed me the gleaming, bottle-green Raleigh bicycle they had bought for me.

It was Uncle Jim who took on the task of teaching me to ride it, confining my first wobbly efforts to the safety of the blue-brick yard that ran alongside the bakehouse building at No 17 Willes Road. Only when he was sufficiently satisfied with my progress did we move out through the big double gates and on into Lansdowne Street. Today, this is a bit of a rat run for those wanting to avoid the traffic lights at the Clarendon Street and Willes Road junctions, but in those days, it was a quiet back street, rarely visited by motor vehicles except for the occasional van or lorry delivering to one of the tiny shops that lined it on both sides. It was a safe enough place for a young girl learning to ride her bike and offered a good stretch of road to practice on.

Soon we were travelling further and further afield, until came the day when Uncle decided that I could ride well enough now to go as far as Waverley Woods. All went well on the outward journey with Uncle riding beside me offering a steadying hand on the shoulder from time to time. It was my first visit to the woods and I was enchanted by them, but perhaps it was a journey too far for that young girl, for as we cycled past the Midland Oak on our way home, my front wheel wobbled into Uncle's front wheel and suddenly we were both sent sprawling across the road. Fortunately, the car travelling behind us was going sufficiently slowly to stop and the driver waited patiently as we picked ourselves up - but I never saw the bike again!

The two uncles were my mother's younger brothers and at the time of the bicycle incident, Uncle Jim, the elder of the two, was living with his wife and their baby daughter in a tiny cottage at No 1 Lansdowne Road. It was just as well that his wife got on with her mother-in-Law, for Granny lived next door at No 2. The two households shared both the toilet at the end of the yard, and the washhouse opposite where a cast iron pump over the sink held endless fascination for my sister and me.

In spite of its name, Lansdowne Road was actually nothing more than a narrow service passage providing rear access to the buildings in Lansdowne and Clarendon Streets, and the casual observer glancing down the entrance in passing, would almost certainly have been unaware that it was also home to six tiny cottages and two workshops. Numbers 1 and 2 belonged to the Wallsgrove Brothers (Builders) and I would often be sent to pay the rent at their offices just round the corner in Leicester Street.

The previous year, Uncle Tom had married Beatrice, daughter of George and Winifred Cashmore, who owned the bakery and shop that wrapped themselves around the corner of No 17 Willes Road and Lansdowne Street. All four worked in the business and, together with Auntie's younger brother, Georgie, lived amiably 'above shop`. It was here that I would find myself living for most of 1951, whilst my mother recovered from the birth of my brother.

The aunts and uncles were up early, easing their bodies out of their beds to start the day's labours at such a time of morning that would see many of today's young people still making their way home from the town's nightclubs; and by the time I woke up and crawled out of my own cosy bed, the air would be heavily scented with the delicious aroma of baking bread.

On Saturdays, I loved to creep into the bakehouse and settle myself down in a corner to watch the uncles at work, finding a certain fascination in watching Uncle Tom's strong, muscular arms kneading the great swollen mounds of dough into submission, before taking a sharp knife and cutting it into pieces ready to be placed into baking tins.

Sometimes he would vary the procedure by shaping the dough into long, fat torpedoes and slashing deep cuts into the tops; As if by magic these would slowly open up and spread themselves wide as the bread rose. Another time he might choose to make cottage loaves, forming some of the dough into large squashy balls and the rest of it into slightly smaller but equally squashy rounds. Then he would take one of the smaller pieces, place it on top of a bigger one and plunge a floured finger right down through the middle thus sealing them together.

When the loaves were sufficiently swollen, Uncle George would take charge, arranging them, pale and white, on the end of a big wooden paddle and thrusting it through the gaping jaws of the bread oven. Shortly afterwards, he would retrieve them again, now beautifully golden-brown and crusty, and tantalizingly tempting.

When I tired of watching the uncles, I might go in search of the aunts, who were usually to be found in the kitchen or in the tiny finishing room behind the shop. This was where the cakes, still naked from the oven, were given the decorative coatings that made them more tempting to the customers. Some, like the iced finger, needed nothing more than a generous coat of icing spread along its length, but its rotund cousin, the Devonshire split, demanded a more luxurious finish, and so a deep cut would be made in the top and the resultant gap filled with a generous helping of jam and cream. Finally, a sprinkling of icing sugar would be shaken over the top.

If a person's fancy leaned more towards the cup cake, then they might choose one which was simply finished by a coat of white icing, with a small sugar flower placed on top, or, then again, they might prefer the butterfly cake. This started life in the same way as the cup cake, but in the finishing room the top would be cut off in such a way as to leave a small depression to be filled with butter cream. The top would then be cut in two and arranged on the cream to resemble a pair of butterfly wings. Again, a sprinkling of icing sugar would provide the finishing touch.

Other cakes such as the éclair or the Viennese finger, required a dressing of chocolate, but some, such as the rock cake, the almond tart and the deliciously fruity, buttery, Chelsea bun, needed no decoration, satisfying both the eyes and the palate without need for any adornments.

One spring morning, Auntie and I set off on a train journey to London to meet up with her friend, Ann, who was a nurse at one of the hospitals. Had they not been accompanied by the young me then perhaps the two ladies would have been content to simply spend the day browsing the shops, but for that particular day they had chosen London Zoo as our destination. Crossing Regent's Park, I delighted in watching the antics of the squirrels dashing back and forth across the grass and scampering up into the trees, little knowing that within minutes I was about to be totally charmed by the sight of the most famous baby in Britain.

Brumas was the cute polar bear cub who had been born at the zoo in November 1949. The first polar bear to be successfully raised there, her arrival seems to have attracted the kind of excitement that is usually given to a Royal birth and people were flocking to the zoo in their millions hoping to get a glimpse of her.

It was an exciting day; my first ever trip to a zoo and I was fascinated to be seeing for real, so many of the animals that I had hitherto only seen in picture books, but today my only other clear memory of our visit sees me being strapped into a long wooden seat along with several other children, and being taken for an elephant ride around the zoo gardens.

If the visit to London had been exciting, then the prospect of a trip to the seaside was even more so. Perhaps a different place would have been chosen if Auntie and Uncle had known that come low tide at Weston-Super-Mare, the sea retreats to such a distance that it becomes nothing more than a blur on the horizon. Thus, it was on our arrival. I have vague memories of playing on the beach, but the real highlight of the day came when we boarded a coach and joined an excursion to Wookey Hole Caves in the Mendip Hills.

Joining the group of people waiting at the entrance, we followed our guide into the darkness, slowly making our way deeper and deeper into the caves. Every now and then we would pause while he illuminated areas of particular interest or told us a little of the caves' history. "The bones of pre-historic and tropical animals had been found in the caves", he told us; "animals such as hyenas, lions and bears, and they had even found "... here he had paused a moment for effect..." the complete skeleton of a woman!"

Down Hell's Ladder we went, emerging into a huge chamber with a river running across the far end of it. The guide continued with his commentary; this was as far as we could go, he explained, for although there were other passages and chambers to explore, they lay under water and could only be reached by divers. Then he turned us round and pointing to an enormous stalagmite, delivered his pièce de résistance. This," he told us dramatically," is the Witch of Wookey."

"Long, long ago," he went on," she had lived in the caves with her little dog, but she was not liked by the villagers who accused her of casting spells whenever anything went wrong for them. Eventually, a monk was sent to exorcise her and he chased her through the caves and into the cavern. There he blessed a handful of river water and threw it over her, whereupon she instantly turned to stone... along with her little dog" he added, pointing to a smaller stalagmite at the Witches feet. Caves and witches... what could be more exciting for a seven-year-old child?

Life at No 17 had an easy rhythm to it. The Aunts and Uncles had a business to run and had developed a routine that saw their days running satisfyingly smoothly. All they expected of me was that I should fit into that routine and cause as little disruption as possible. I was at school for much of the time, of course, and then I would go to play with a friend before heading back to No 17 in time to help set the table with delicate bone china cups & saucers, ready for tea. This task was not complete until I had taken a large plate into the shop and selected six cakes from those left over after the day's trading had ceased.

The meal over, Auntie Beat and I would set off to take Laddie, their beautiful red setter, for a walk over the Campion Hills. One evening we returned to find Aunt Winnie settled comfortably in her chair, knitting a pair of ankle socks which, it turned out, she intended for me. They were white, with a turn-over top worked in a blue and white chequer-board pattern. Still struggling at the holey dishcloth stage of the craft myself, I was astonished to find Auntie not only knitting simultaneously with four needles, but with two different coloured yarns also. I was deeply impressed. WOW! How did she do that?

In fact, both aunts were excellent needle-women and when they were not busy knitting, they might well be found dressmaking, using the old treadle sewing machine that stood beneath the sitting room window. This intrigued me. How could rocking a metal platform with your feet down there, result in a beautifully neat row of stitches appearing beneath your hands at table level?

For all that they worked so long and hard, the aunts & uncles were always very kind and patient with the young niece who had invaded their world; I cannot recall any one of them ever getting cross with me, although they must have been sorely tempted at times as I wandered into the bake house and finishing room to watch them at work. I adored them all, but my mother was well again now and Auntie was expecting a baby of her own. It was time for me to go home... and after my brief taste of luxury, I was about to be bought back down to earth with a rather big bump.

Chapter Three
Number Twenty Park Street

A few clicks of the mouse and there it was – a black and white aerial photograph of No 20 Park Street, the house where I was born & raised. Though long gone now - demolished under the slum clearance programme of the 1950's and 60's - in my mind it stands there still, as solid as it ever was.

A tall, narrow, red-brick building set halfway along the street, on its northern side it was attached, top to bottom, to a house that was almost its mirror image; however, on its southern elevation, only the top two storeys were to be found pressed up against its neighbour, thus forming a narrow passage betwixt the two buildings at ground level.

The house was arranged on three floors with two rooms on each and an unlit staircase; steep and narrow, running sharply upwards through its centre. This paused briefly at the halfway point to form a narrow landing just one door-width wide, before continuing upwards again until it encountered the outer wall of the house. There, as if uncertain where to go next, it split itself neatly into two and turned, simultaneously, to both left and right, leading one into the two top-floor rooms.

Below ground level was a double cellar, dark and scary; visited only when necessity demanded it; to fetch coal, perhaps, or to put a large brown penny in the gas meter. My mother used to tell of the time she reached out into the gloom to pick up a piece of coal, only to find something warm and soft and furry move beneath her fingers. She jumped back in fright, convinced it was a rat, and was very relieved then to discover that, after all, it was only our family cat, which had chosen the pile of coal on which to have a snooze.

We shared the house with my father's nephew, George; his wife, Marge; and their two sons, Ray and John; who were about the same ages as Pat and myself. A tall well-built man, George worked at the Ford Foundry and would sometimes bring home shiny, silver ball-bearings for his sons to play with, which made them the envy of we other children during games of marbles.

Marge, as I remember, was much shorter than George. A round, jolly young woman who laughed a lot, she had reddish, curly hair and seemed always to have on a full face of brightly coloured make-up that somehow seemed perfectly right for her cheerful persona. George and company occupied the two top-floor rooms and one of the rooms on the middle floor, the one that overlooked the blue-bricked back yard and dilapidated out-buildings. We used the other three rooms.

In an earlier life, the building had been a bakery and the old bakehouse was still there across the yard. We children were not allowed in there as it was judged too unsafe, but I have distant memories of standing in the doorway watching my mother stirring the contents of a large grey pot on the cooker. At some point in my childhood, the cooker was moved into the back ground-floor room of the house, along with a large kitchen table and an assortment of old kitchen chairs, and then the battered old bakery door was closed and locked forever.

Sandwiched between the bakehouse and the neighbouring Salvation Army Citadel, was a narrow passageway that led to an unkempt patch of ground where, at various times, my father kept chickens and rabbits which were almost certainly destined, eventually, for the pot. He also tried his hand with homing pigeons but this was to be a very short-lived hobby for, as my mother often related with great glee, the first time he let them out, they rose up into the clear blue sky, circled round, then disappeared from view, never to be seen again!

It was here also that our lavatory was to be found, tucked neatly into a corner behind the bakehouse. As we didn't have electricity, there was no light, and so it was that on dark nights, a candle was taken to light the way, one hand carefully cupped around the fragile flame lest a playful breeze should suddenly happen along and plunge one into darkness. The wise person would be careful to tuck a few pages of yesterday's newspaper under his arm before embarking on the journey betwixt house and toilet, for one could never be certain of finding a supply of this most necessary of necessities already in situ, swinging from the nail put there long ago for just that purpose. Toilet paper was available, but it was horribly scratchy and not very absorbent, being more akin to tracing paper than a product intended for use on those tender parts of the anatomy.

Understandably, no-one wanted to get out of bed and make the long journey to the outside lavatory in the middle of the night and so, should nature call, we used a chamber pot. This was a bowl-shaped vessel with a handle attached at the side, much like those we use for potty-training small children today, and could be made from enamel, earthenware, or ceramics. The enamel version, being the cheapest, was the model most likely to be found in the poorest homes but whilst durable and easy to clean, the enamel could easily be chipped, so care had to be taken when using it. Next in the pecking order came the earthenware version. Plain and unadorned, this seemed to come in any colour you liked – as long as it was white! The most desirable were the ceramic pots, which came highly decorated. Usually these featured elaborate bouquets of painted flowers around the outside, but those with a naughty sense of humour might choose one printed inside with a saucy verse, or even a large eye that stared up unblinkingly from the bottom, as one performed.

The pots were known by a variety of names; the po, the pot, the potty; the piss pot, the jerry or the gozunder. In most houses they were simply kept under the bed, but some homes boasted a small pot cupboard in which to hide it away when not in use. If you were 'real posh', however, you might use a commode. This was a wooden framed armchair with a loose top seat which could be removed to reveal another seat below with a hole cut into it, designed to hold a chamber pot.

In 1849, a cholera outbreak hit the town with Williams and Johns Courts in Satchwell Street being named as the most seriously affected. A Health Board report states that both Courts were filthy, with unfenced receptacles (cess pits) for waste, into which small children could easily fall. It was also noted that the residents complained of not having any water. These two courts were immediately behind nos.18 and 20 Park Street.

By the time I was born however, sanitation levels throughout the town were greatly improved, even so the only water supply for the whole of No 20 was provided by just one cold tap in the washhouse; a brick-built outbuilding with whitewashed walls, unlit and unheated except on wash day, when the brick copper in one corner would be filled with bucket after bucket of cold water, and a fire lit in the stoke-hole bellow.

The weekly wash was hard work involving a great deal of scrubbing at the shallow stone sink, followed by boiling, rinsing, and rinsing again until mom was finally satisfied that all the soap had been removed. The whites would then be given a final rinse, this time with a blue bag* added to the water, in order to turn us all out looking whiter than white, brighter than bright.

When the rinsing was complete, the washing was put into a large metal bath and taken out into the yard where an enormous cast iron mangle stood waiting to receive it between two massive rollers. When my sister and I were at home we were enlisted to help with this task, one of us struggling to turn the heavy handle, the other catching the flattened clothes as they emerged from between the rollers. Finally, the clothes were firmly pegged to a washing line and, like a row of nautical flags, would then be hoisted aloft to shake themselves dry.

Baths were taken in a long metal tub brought in from the wash house and placed on the kitchen floor. Meantime, water would be heated on top of the cooker in the big metal pot my mother used for making stews. When judged to be hot enough, this would be emptied into the bath tub together with several buckets of cold water and in we would climb, Pat at one end and me at the other. The lifebuoy washing soap my mother used for the laundry now did service as toilet soap and shampoo, unless there was an outbreak of nits at school, in which case a cake of foul-smelling carbolic soap was used instead, followed by a thorough combing with a fine-tooth comb.

Perhaps In order to avoid making extra washing for herself by using a pretty fabric tablecloth, Mom would simply cover the table with newspaper. This could be left in place for days, until she finally noticed that it was looking a bit grubby or, perhaps, until the parents simply tired of re-reading yesterday's news, then it would be gathered up and replaced by fresh pages of 'The Mirror'. The old 'tablecloth' would not be thrown out, however. Instead, it would be put on one side and perhaps used to light the fire the following day. Indeed, old newspapers were never thrown away; some would be torn into squares and hung on the old nail in the outside lavatory to be used as toilet paper, while any spare ones would be periodically collected together and taken to the fish and chip shop across the road, where they would be warmly welcomed and used to wrap the customers fish 'n' chips.

In those days of 'waste not, want not', nothing was thrown away if some other use could be found for it. Thus, every piece of string that came into the house would be carefully unravelled and stored away, whilst brown paper and paper bags would be carefully folded and placed in a drawer ready to be re-used. Clothes would be mended and darned, until they were no longer considered wearable, after which they would be turned into dusters, used for patching, cut into pieces to serve as handkerchiefs, or be made into rag-rugs. And if they were of no use for any of these purposes, then they would be pushed into a bag and sold for a few precious pennies at the rag shop in Guy Street, but only after buttons and any other useful bits and pieces had been removed.

My mother never did lose the habit of reusing, and after we moved to Lillington, she started donating our newspapers to the local scout troop, who would sell them to raise money for scouting activities. The trouble was that Mom just didn't seem to know when to stop, and long after they were no longer needed, she still went on collecting them.

Unfortunately, she seemed to lack any sense of order and anything she put 'safely' away might never again see the light of day. Such was the case with my Waterman fountain pen. A much-treasured gift from Auntie Beat & Uncle Tom, I had accidently left it on the kitchen table when packing my satchel for school one day. That evening, Mum readily admitted finding the pen and putting it safely away, but just where had she put it? That she couldn't remember and to this day I never saw the pen again.

Although sometimes frustrating, one advantage of Mom's squirreling things away is that I now have possession of her paper 'junk'. Although of no monetary value, it does give fascinating glimpses of the family's past and has proved very useful for researching the family history... but to get back to No 20.

Our other ground floor room was used as the sitting room. In the past, it had been the baker's shop and there were still reminders of this in the neat shelving unit built into one alcove. On these my mother displayed her treasures; an impressive model galleon in full sail and, on the very top shelf, a glass-fronted case holding a stuffed cock pheasant.

Three worn stone steps led from the pavement to the front door which was painted an odd shade of reddish brown; and had a large square window set into the top half. This my mother had covered with a brightly patterned 'stained glass' paper in order to shield us from the prying eyes of passers-by.

At one side of the door, a large bay window stretched across the remainder of the front wall. Coming home from school for lunch one day, I was shocked to discover that the bay had disappeared during my absence, and now there was nothing betwixt the sitting room and the street but an enormous hole! Later, this was partially bricked up and rendered, and a flat, lifeless, modern window inserted. Aesthetically, it wasn't a patch on the old bay as it simply lacked the charm and character.

The front room was home to the family's wireless set, a large brown Bakelite box that sat on top of the drop-leaf table with the beautiful barley-twist legs. This I recall being powered by a huge dry battery, as big as a sizeable hardback book, together with an accumulator. This was a glass jar filled with acid – very like a car battery but half the size – and just like a car battery, it would lose its charge over time. When this happened, it would be taken to the wireless shop in Regent Street to be re-charged. What this meant in practice, was that we would hand over the old accumulator and be given in exchange one that was already charged, for which we would pay a few pennies. Unbelievably, as a small child I was often sent on this errand with a warning to, "be careful you don't drop it." ringing in my ears. It horrifies me now to think what could have happened had I tripped, or the jar slipped from my small fingers.

The wireless was the main form of entertainment for most families. Television was available but was way beyond the means of the working-class home – and, in any case, many houses were still without electricity. We didn't put the wireless on merely to provide background noise as so often happens today, but would tune in for specific programmes. For Mom, there would be 'Housewives Choice' – a music request programme; or the radio soap, 'Mrs Dale's Diary', which told of the everyday comings and goings of Dr Jim Dale and his family. It was very gentle and tame compared with the television soaps of today, but very popular with the womenfolk who tuned in daily to listen over the mid-morning cuppa. My Gran loved, 'The Archers – An Everyday Story of Country Folk', which can still be heard today. Should we be visiting when the programme was on, then we would be made to sit in silence or sent outside to play quietly. Pat and I listened to, 'Lost in Space' and 'Dick Barton – Special Agent', and my dad would tune in for the horse racing and the football results.

He liked to have a little flutter on the horses, writing his choice – always in pencil – on a scrap of paper, and then tightly wrapping it around his stake money ready for my mother to take to the bookie's shop in Clarendon Street. Bookmaking was illegal in those days and so Mom would surreptitiously hand over her little package without a word being exchanged. I'm sure the local bobbies must have known what was going on, but if they did, then they simply turned a blind eye to it. Dad did The Pools every week too, dreaming of what he would do with his big win just like thousands of other folks up and down the country, but the big win never did come, of course.

We all slept in our only bedroom on the middle floor; Pat sleeping in the big double bed with our parents, while I slept my early years away in the cot tucked away in one corner. This was painted pink but the various chips and scratches revealed glimpses of green and black paints beneath. No doubt some of the damage was done by teething babies chomping on the cool metal frame so, given that so many paints were lead–based at that time, we would almost certainly have ingested a generous dose of the metal during our early years. Later, after Tom was born, he was given possession of the cot and I joined Pat in the middle of our parents' bed.

It was some time after I joined Pat that we woke up one morning to find a huge hole in the ceiling above us. It seems that whilst she was getting ready for bed the previous evening, a rotten floorboard had given way beneath Aunt Marge causing her lower half to pay an unexpected visit to our family boudoir below! Fortunately, she didn't seem to have suffered any serious injury and for all that it was such a frightening experience, it worked out in favour of everyone, since shortly after this our cousins moved out into a council house at Whitnash and our parents took possession of their vacated rooms. My mother acquired two cast-iron beds - well worn, with parts of the sprung bases tied together with string - and Pat and I moved in.

Living in the slums, we tended to get very small, unwanted visitors in our beds and, in an attempt to eradicate them, every morning Mom would take a bottle, just like those used in the fish and chip shops for salt & vinegar, and liberally sprinkle DDT** over our mattresses.

If there was a light in our bedroom, then I don't remember it. In any case, we used a candle to light our way up the narrow stairs to bed and this, together with the glow from the street lamp outside our window, provided sufficient illumination for our needs. In wintertime, the beds would be heated by metal hot-water bottles, thickly wrapped in towels or jumpers to protect us from burns. Extra warmth would be provided by Dad's heavy great coat issued to him, I believe, as part of his Dads' Army uniform. If it was really cold, an oil-heater might be lit in an effort to take the chill from the air.

In the alcove opposite to the foot of my cot, stood a wardrobe with a long, mirrored door; a door with which, for a time, I became very well acquainted. It came about because, like most small children, I was fascinated by the grown-up's ability to wink, and I desperately wanted to be able to perform this most wonderful feat for myself. To this end, I would spend hours in front of that door, pulling the most horrendous faces at my reflection as I struggled to accomplish this!

A low cupboard stood in a second alcove and on this was displayed my parents' small collection of books. Most are long forgotten but a few have always stayed in my mind; 'She' by Rider Haggard, and a large blue book of The Scriptures, which had the names and dates of birth of all my mother's siblings listed inside the front cover; Coffins' Botanic Guide to Health was also to be found there, and, most surprisingly of all, a slim green volume on the subject of algebra. The last has always puzzled me. Mom and Dad were never educated beyond basic arithmetic, so how on earth did they come to possess such a book - and why?

During the late nineteen fifties onwards, most of the buildings in Satchwell Street, together with those on the western side of Park Street, were demolished under the slum clearance programme. For many years afterwards, the land served as a rough car park, but in the early 1980's, the Royal Priors Shopping Centre was built there, The design for this included a row of small shops in Park Street, one of which, numbered No 20, stands in exactly the same place as the No 20 where I was born.

(*BLUE BAGS: About the size of a cotton reel and made of muslin, the blue bags were filled with a mix of ultramarine and bicarb of soda, and were designed to remove any yellowness caused by the washing soap.

**DDT (Dichlorodiphenyltrichloroethane)
A powerful insecticide which was used by the American Military during the Second World War, to protect against insect-born infections such as typhus and malaria.
Following the War, it was released for use by the general public but concerns soon arose over its safety and it was banned in Britain in 1986, and then World Wide by the Stockholm Convention in 2001.)

Chapter Four

How to Release a Head Stuck in Railings

Had you asked me back in the days when we were living there - and had I known the meaning of the word - I would have told you that Park Street was residential, so many were the people who called it home but, in fact, it also accommodated a large and surprisingly diverse number of businesses.

On the west side of the street, at number two, Arnold Tunnicliff could be found working at his craft of picture framer behind the painted-out windows of his shop; these, perhaps, a relic of the war years and the blackout. On the other hand, Harry Lovell, the neighbouring seed merchant, boasted a window that was light and bright and seemed always to include hen's eggs in its display, nestled on top of a pile of golden straw.

Next was Mrs Olorenshaw's second-hand furniture store. Our friend lived with her parents in one tiny room at the top of this building, until the Council finally moved them into a prefab at the top of the Campion Hills. What luxury that must have seemed. And, indeed, it was a very nice little house with lots of room, a garden, and the whole of Leamington spread out before it in the valley below.

One of the most unusual businesses was Legge's, the sheet metal workers at number eight. Today, they would almost certainly be found on an industrial estate but such oddities were not at all unusual in the Leamington backstreets of my childhood.

The largest shop in the street was Arthur Barr & Sons, petroleum merchants; china, glass and hardware dealers, who were to be found at Numbers 12 & 14. In fact, they sold a great deal more than that and it was to here that I might be dispatched when Mom needed a packet of Tide washing powder or a bluebag for her washing; or perhaps a packet of firelighters to help get the fire going.

According to Kelly's Directory for 1945, Charles Organ - tailor, was occupying Number 16, but by 1953 it is his wife Clara, a dressmaker, who is listed there as a wardrobe dealer, and it is she who I remember. A little lady who wore round-rimmed glasses and arranged her hair in a coiled plait on top of her head, she still favoured the long ankle-skimming skirts of an earlier generation. In my memory, the large window to the right of the door is always covered by generous black curtains. Although also serving as blackout blinds, I imagine they had originally been put there to preserve the modesty of the clients as they were measured for new clothes. On the other hand, the smaller window to the left was always uncovered to let the daylight in and provided a cosy daytime home for their little Yorkshire terrier, who seemed to spend his every day snoozing there on a nice plump cushion.

If you had walked straight past No's 18 and 20 you would then have found yourself outside the Salvation Army Citadel, an imposing, castellated building, and the largest in the street. It was here that we went to Sunday school and where we gathered together in a back room on one evening a week, to play games such as spin the bottle or musical chairs. Those who attended Sunday school regularly for one whole year were rewarded with books. I was never to achieve that myself but my sister had several books, two of which I remember well; one was an illustrated copy of The Water Babies by Charles Kingsley, whilst the other contained a selection of Fairy Tales by Hans Christian Andersen. However, Pat wasn't much of a one for the reading and it was my hands that were more likely to be found turning the pages of the books.

It was whilst attending Sunday school here that I was first introduced to the pheasant's eye narcissus, when each child was handed one flower to take home to our mothers on Mothering Sunday, along with a colourfully illustrated bible tract.

It was this building that also provided the opportunity for me to give myself the fright of my young life. It came about when, unseen by my mother, I had managed to twist open the big heavy knob on the front door for the first time, and let myself out onto the top step.

I stood there for a few moments surveying the other two steps below. I really wanted to jump over them just as I had seen my sister do so many times, but the footpath seemed so far away... Courage failed me and so, reluctantly, I moved down to the middle step. Again, I hesitated and again my courage failed... Now I was standing on the bottom step. Dare I? Dare I? Taking a deep breath, I launched myself into the air...

Picking myself up off the pavement, I turned and looked down the street to where Pat and her friends were playing. They were taking it in turns to scramble through a gap in the railings that fronted the Salvation Army building and swinging, trapeze fashion, from a metal bar that secured the railings to the wall beyond.

I watched them for a while then decided that I wanted to join in too and so, without anyone noticing what I was doing, I toddled over to the railings and pushed my head between the nearest two bars. Then I tried to squeeze my body after it just as I had seen the other children do, but to my puzzlement it wouldn't go. I squirmed and I pushed, and then I s-q-u-i-r-med some more – but it was no good, no matter how hard I tried the body stubbornly refused to follow the head. Eventually I gave up, but when I tried to withdraw my head something very strange happened, for the young head that had pushed through so easily just moments earlier, was now refusing to be pulled out and I was well and truly trapped!

My frightened cries alerted the other children and immediately they were swarming round me. Someone took me by the waist and pulled while someone else took hold of my head and pushed. Push, pull... Push, pull...but the only thing all that pushing and pulling achieved was to make the hard metal bars bite into the flesh behind my ears, making me cry even louder. Someone fetched my mother. "Oh, ower Val, what 'ave you done now?" she said, before she, in turn, took hold of my waist and pulled; the metal bars took another bite at me and I yelled louder still.

42

By now other grown-ups had come to see what all the noise was about and as I sobbed, they discussed how to set me free. It was my ears that were causing the problem, someone suggested; they were sticking out too much. A boy was instructed to hold the offending appendages flat against my head whilst my mother again tried to tug me free. They tried turning my head to one side in an attempt to free just one ear at a time and when that failed, they tried turning the head the opposite way and freeing the other ear instead, but no matter what they tried, I remained firmly stuck. Everyone fell silent as they contemplated what to do next, then a woman's voice spoke. "Rub a bit of butter on 'er ears, it'll make 'em slippy an' she'll slide out then alright."

Everyone seemed to agree that this was a good idea and so that precious commodity was brought out and a goodly dollop roughly massaged into my ears. Once more the boy clamped his hands over them, and once more someone gripped me round the waist and pulled...but all to no avail, I remained firmly trapped with my head sticking out on one side of the railing, and my bottom sticking out on the other. Again, everyone fell silent, and then someone had a real brainwave. "Send fer Charlie, 'e'll know what to do."

Charlie Rodgers owned the fish and chip shop opposite to our house, but he also worked as an auxiliary fireman*. One of the boys was sent to fetch him and within moments I could hear his cheerful voice." Now then Valerie, what have you been up to?" With that he took me in his strong fireman arms and simply turned me over by 180 degrees, before gently easing my head back through the bars. Out it popped as easily as it gone in all those endless minutes before!

Next door to the Citadel was a narrow passageway leading to a row of three tiny cottages tucked away behind No 26 Park Street and known as Albert Place. The Doust School of Motoring was to be found there at No 1, one of only three Driving Schools listed for Leamington Spa in 1953.

Mrs Haynes ran a second-hand clothes shop from the front room of No 28 and I remember my mother sending me there one day to see if the good lady had any shoes to fit me. She listened to what I had to say, then simply waved her hand towards the pile of shoes in a corner and told me to see if I could find anything there. At first there didn't seem to be anything suitable but then I spotted them right down at the bottom of the pile - a pair of bright red leather shoes with neat rounded toes and a dainty strap that stretched across the foot to fasten with a shiny, red ball button. They were beautiful and I fell in love with them in an instant. What is more they fitted perfectly. In a moment I was out of the door excitedly clutching the shoes to my chest as I rushed home to show my find to Mom, but to my puzzlement she frowned deeply as she took them from me and turned them over in her hands. "These are no good," she said "They're tap shoes, they'll 'ave t' go back." And that was the last I saw of those pretty red shoes.

The large windows that fronted No's 30–34, suggested that they had originally been built as shops but by 1953 only D H Rawlings, woodworker and cabinet maker, is shown to be working there, at No 34.

Gladys Lee, a tiny ladies hairdressing salon, occupied No 36, the various lotions and potions used within; perfuming the air outside her shop each time the door was opened. Usually when I was deemed to be in need of a haircut, this would be done by a young woman living opposite, but I do remember on one occasion being sent to Gladys Lee for a semi shingle. How grown-up it felt to be having my hair done at a proper hairdressing salon, although I've long forgotten what a semi-shingle looks like.

Although there is an early school photograph showing Pat with short bobbed hair, she seems to have escaped the hair cutting for most of her childhood since I can only ever remember her wearing it long. Sometimes it would be arranged in one plait reaching down the middle of her back, but on other days it would be divided in two with the plaits left lying loosely across her shoulders or twisted up and fastened neatly on top of her head. I was always envious of her long tresses but Mom would never allow me to grow my hair long as she considered that having one head of long hair to cope with in the mornings was more than enough. At least the boys couldn't tie me to a lamp post by my hair, as our mother often claimed they did with Pat when she annoyed them one day!

Both my sisters had curly blonde hair when young but they must have mislaid that mould when I was made, because I had neither the blonde curls nor even the jet-black hair so prevalent in both parental families. Mom always said that I was auburn-haired but I just saw myself as a rather drab mouse. What cannot be disputed is my father's observation that my hair was as straight as a yard of pump water.

The last of the buildings in the row housed Stratton's Carpet Cleaning business on the ground floor. Huge sliding doors opened onto a passageway at the side of the building and I would often slip down there to watch the men at work, furiously scrubbing soapy suds into the carpets with long-handled brushes, before hosing them down with copious amounts of water and hoisting them up into the rafters to drip dry.

On the corner stood Godfrey's bakery which had its shop in Regent Street and the bakehouse, with its ever-open door, in Park Street. Long after everyone else had moved on to motorised transport, Mr Godfrey could still be seen around town delivering his orders by pony and trap. When not out doing the rounds, the pony would stand patiently outside the bakehouse, head buried deep in its nosebag.

Thus it was on one warm summer day, some men working on a building nearby, let down the back of their tip-up truck and deposited a load of bricks on the road with such a crash, that the poor pony was startled. It reared up on its hind legs and would surely have galloped off had not the chocks placed beneath the trap's wheels, prevented it from doing so. Concerned for the pony, and quite oblivious of the danger I might be putting myself in, I started to run towards it, intent only to calm it down. Fortunately, Mr Godfrey came out of the bakehouse at that moment and shouted at me to stay away before he, himself, went to the animal to settle it.

We didn't have cakes very often but every once in a while, Mom would hand over some coins and send me to Godfrey's shop to get three farthings worth of stale cakes. In return for our money a large paper bag would be crammed to bursting with the previous day's leftovers, and handed across the counter to us with the same levels of politeness that would be shown to any other customer. Yesterday's cakes they may have been but we considered them excellent value for money and a real treat.

Generally speaking, the buildings on the east side of the street were somewhat smaller than those on the western side and many had quite obviously been built originally as residential properties. Some can still be found there today, though much altered, so that a tiny cottage that was once home to a family might now be converted into retail premises and be trading as an upmarket boutique.

But going back now to my childhood days: Cecil B Croft ran his cycle shop from No 49, close to the corner with Regent Street, then came a number of neat little houses of various designs, the last of these, somewhat incongruously, sitting cheek by jowl with B & B Trailers, who made caravan chassis and accessories. Most of the time we would be unaware of their presence but every once in a while, the big green doors would be opened and a strange metal contraption carefully manoeuvred into the narrow street.

In complete contrast, neighbouring Miss Rule was the Hon. Secretary of the Royal Air Forces Association (Leamington Spa Branch 310) which she ran quietly from her home at No 35, adjacent to a set of four tiny back-to-back houses.

Pat used to run errands for two elderly ladies living in one pair. To my young eyes they appeared to be of similar age, but they were very different in appearance. Gentle faced, one had snow white hair, short and curly, and wore the styles of the day, her dress covered by a colourful wrap-around apron to protect it as she went about her daily chores. In contrast, the other lady habitually wore clothes from an earlier era consisting of a long-sleeved black blouse with a high neck, together with a voluminous skirt of the same colour, from which protruded the toes of a pair of black buttoned boots. She had quite sharp features and wore her still dark hair in a bun at the base of her neck. I thought she looked like a witch and kept my distance but Pat had no such fears and would visit both ladies after school. Imagine her shock then, when she pushed open the door one day and found the witch lady lying dead at the foot of her stairs.

Attached to the other side of the back-to-backs was a small grocery shop to which my mother would send me when she wanted a tin of Bachelor's processed peas or a packet of Foster-Clark's oxtail soup powder to flavour a stew. Today, Mr Davis might be considered something of an entrepreneur since he had converted an old ambulance into a mobile shop which he used to tour around the local villages.

At No 27, the Kimberley's would allow their second-hand goods to escape through the open door and spill out onto the pavement. Every once in a while, kind Mrs Kimberley would hand over a small bundle of American comics to whichever child might be playing in the street; a rare treat, these would be eagerly read from cover to cover and passed around until everyone had had their fill, then we would collect them all together and take them to another second-hand shop in Regent Street, where we would exchange them for a precious penny or two.

Living next door to the bric-a-brac shop was a boy I only ever caught glimpses of, as he came and went dressed in his Leamington Boy's College uniform; in all the years he never once spoke, just quietly came and went and ignored all the other children completely.

Of all the shops in the street, Mr Harrison's newsagents was the one that held the most interest for we children, since the window would always contain a variety of small pocket-money toys such as colouring pencils, small rubber balls and plasticine; notebooks and weirdly-shaped five stones. If a measuring ruler was needed then there would be a choice of two sizes – a neat little six-inch affair, or a larger, and more expensive, twelve inch. Marbles also came in two types; those which were made from clay and coated in the dullest shades of red, or blue or green paint; and those which were made from brightly coloured glass.

49

The clay variety was the least popular since it tended to chip easily and some children would refuse to play for them, preferring the more colourful glass variety.

Two doors away from the newsagents was Charlie's Fish and Chip shop, where the newspapers sold by Mr Harrison on any one day, might well be found the next, now being used as wrapping for a tasty portion of cod and chips. Today's fish & chip shop will offer a variety of meals and you might choose cod, haddock or plaice to accompany your fried potatoes. Then again, you might prefer chicken, or a pie, or a battered sausage; a vegetable croquette or a frankfurter. If none of these tickle your fancy, then perhaps a beef burger, a veggie burger or a kebab will fit the bill... and there will always be a selection of spicy sauces on offer. Back in the day, however, most chippies sold nothing more than the basic fish and chip meal, with mushy green peas offered as a side dish perhaps.

The Globe was a tiny pub run by Charles Naylor and sometimes favoured by my father for an evening pint. If we peered round the door at him – and he was in a generous mood – then he might buy us a glass of lemonade and a packet of crisps. These came in just one flavour, plain ordinary potato, with a screw of blue waxed paper containing salt for those who wanted something a little tastier.

Watson's Furniture Removers could be found close to the Warwick Street junction, and it was they who would move us when the time finally came for us to leave Park Street. For a while my father's cousin, Freda Goddard, ran the small general stores at No 5, but by 1953 this had changed hands and was now run by Mrs May, whilst a tripe shop occupied No 1. Although my mother would sometimes buy the ghastly-looking chitterlings** from the pork butchers for my father - who seemed to relish them - she had her limitations and tripe was just a dish too far.

Sandwiched between those last two shops was a small cottage occupied by Mr Joe Erswell. Sometimes my mother would cook dinner for him and I would go with her when she took it across. A kindly man, he would encourage me to sing for him and then give me a silver sixpence for doing so, thus helping to foster the misapprehension that I might actually have some talent in this direction!

(*THE FIRE STATION that I remember, was in Adelaide Road down by the river. However, apparently there was also another much larger building in Chandos Street, but I have no recollection of this.

The present fire station can be found in Warwick Street having been built on the site of Beech Lawn, the home of Dr Henry Jephson.

**CHITTERLINGS are pigs' intestines. Thoroughly washed, they are apparently soaked in salt and vinegar and then boiled until soft.)

Chapter Five
An Aromatic Place

The Leamington of my childhood was a far more aromatic place than the town we know today and even with eyes taped tight closed; we would surely have found little difficulty finding our way around, simply by following our noses.

My own journey would have started the moment I opened our front door and found myself breathing in the appetising aromas wafting across the road from the fish and chip shop. Charlie Rodgers and his wife offered satisfyingly chunky chips cooked to perfection in deep vats of sizzling hot fat, accompanied by tender fish encased in a thick overcoat of crispy, crunchy batter; the whole liberally seasoned with salt and vinegar and served, as some would say proper fish and chips should be, in several sheets of old newspaper. Their speciality was the scallop; a thick slice of potato coated with batter and cooked alongside the fish until the middle was soft and light and fluffy. Should anyone have a mind for something a little more exotic, then it was to be had in the form of the pickled eggs, onions and gherkins that sat in obese glass jars at one end of the counter.

If I turned left and headed towards Warwick Street, I would soon find myself passing Arthur Barr's shop with its smells of paraffin & chopped firewood; of candles and laundry soap; the various fragrances all mixing together to form a not unpleasant whole.

Onwards now to the top of the street where, on a hot summer day, my nostrils would be filled with the scent of warm rubber escaping from the open doors of the Normier Tyre shop on the opposite side of the road. In one window a life-sized figure of the Michelin Man could be seen, slowly inflating to almost fill the space allotted to it and then, after a brief pause, gradually deflating again until it was collapsed in a sorry heap on the floor.

Mingling with the smell of rubber were the more appetizing aromas coming from Matthews's pork butcher's shop. Here, it was said, they used every part of the pig except its squeal. In one window, pork chops and sausages sat alongside pig's trotters, brains and chitterlings. Sometimes a whole pig's head would take centre stage, an apple stuffed firmly into its mouth as it gazed out through unseeing eyes onto the world beyond. The other window contained all cooked foods: succulent pork pies, roast pork slices, and sausage rolls; black pudding, faggots and pots of pork dripping, the creamy white fat at the top of the pot concealing the delicious dark jelly lurking beneath.

A few yards on I would pass the chemist's shop with its strange chemical smells. This was a time when pharmacists still mixed a great many of their own lotions and potions in tiny mini-laboratories hidden away at the rear of the shop. It was from here that we bought the jars of minty antacid tablets that Granny took to try and keep her heartburn at bay, and which she sometimes gave to Pat and me as a special treat. From here also came those revolting, yellow sulphur tablets that my mother made me suck to 'clean my blood' the time I broke out in painful boils; and the jars of cod liver oil and malt that my sister loved and I hated.

Further along the street, just past the British & Argentine Meat Company, was The Shoe Hospital; a tiny shoe repair shop that smelled of leather & oil, and of glue & polish. Inside, the cobbler could be seen sitting by the window, head bent over his last, a work-dirtied apron wrapped around him and a row of tiny nails protruding from his mouth. These would be swiftly extracted one by one and used to attach a new leather sole to a shoe.

Most shoes were soled and heeled with leather in those days, but they wore through quickly and getting them repaired was an expensive business. That being so, many families would acquire a shoe last and carry out their own repairs using ready-shaped soles and heels that could be purchased from various shops, as could the cork or leather studs that my father hammered into the bottom of his football boots. These were sturdy leather affairs akin to work boots and far removed from the dainty football boots of today. The cheapest repair, and one which was frequently used for our child-sized footwear, would be to simply stuff the shoes with layers of cardboard!

My father was already in his forties by the time I was born and although I remember his boots quite clearly, I have no recollection whatever of seeing him play. However, there is a photo of the Cubbington football team taken during the 1931 – 32 season, which shows them proudly showing off their trophies.

Next door to the cobbler's was another pork butcher's shop which my mother favoured when she wanted sausages. This was a busy shop and there always seemed to be a lengthy queue. In those days all butcher's shops would have the floors covered in sawdust to absorb any drips and grease and this shop always had a satisfyingly deep layer, just right for me to while away the time as I waited, by drawing pictures and patterns with the toe of my shoe.

At the greengrocer's the produce was so fresh that the air around would be filled with the scents of the various fruits and vegetables. Many were grown locally, coming from the farms and market gardens around and about the town. Labels would proudly announce, 'Kenilworth tomatoes', while others would warn 'Do not squeeze'; or perhaps more politely - 'Please do not squeeze me until I am yours'.

Asparagus, for those who could afford it, came from the Vale of Evesham which, even today, provides 65% of the country's supplies. The Vale also supplied much of our fruit – apples, pears, plums etc. and with the trees in full spring blossom, local coach companies would seize the opportunity to offer afternoon tours.

At harvest time, large woven baskets of plums, damsons and greengages would be on offer for jam making, although one suspects that many of the fruits were simply eaten as they came, for if it is fruit you have a mind for, then what can be more tempting to the taste buds than the prospect of biting into the soft, juice-laden flesh of a fully ripe Victoria plum.

Greengrocers, fishmongers, bakers and butchers; at a time when the arrival of the town's first supermarket was still some years hence, one did not have to venture far to find a food store of one kind or another, each emitting its own distinctive aroma to mix & mingle outside their doors and help to perfume the air of our streets.

Rawlins Bros. (saddlers) Ltd. could be found on The Parade, the strong smell of new leather announcing its location long before one reached the shop. It was to here that Mom and I went in search of my first school satchel only to find that a leather one was priced way beyond her reach. I was happy to settle for one made of canvas, but even that must have put quite a strain on her purse.

Nearby was Tuckers the florist, which surely must have been the smallest shop in town. Sandwiched between Moore's, the confectioners & tobacconists, in Warwick Street, and the rear end of an outfitters' shop on the corner of the Parade, it seemed to consist of nothing more than one tiny display window and a doorway, with precious little space for even one customer to venture inside; however, what it lacked in space was more than compensated for by the fragrant scents escaping from the doorway to totally envelop passers-by, and encourage them to stop and buy.

It was when I stopped to admire the flowers one day, that I noticed a bucket of roses in the doorway with a sign declaring 6d. Now, most days I wouldn't have as much as a farthing in my pocket but on that particular day there just happened to be a silver sixpence lurking there, earned, perhaps, from running errands – or maybe it was a reward from Mr Erswell for entertaining him so nicely with my vocal prowess!

At that time, I had no idea that certain flowers were priced per bloom and the embarrassment on my face must have been obvious as the assistant explained that my 6d would buy me just one single rose and not the whole big bunch I envisaged. 'Are they for mummy?' she asked kindly, 'then let me see if I can find something else for you,' she continued, disappearing into the rear of the shop and returning moments later with a dainty posy of sweet-smelling violets. This was my first close-up encounter with these delicate little flowers and I was instantly charmed; A single rose or a whole bunch of violets blue? There was simply no contest.

The Cadena Cafe could be found on the lower Parade, opposite to the Town Hall. Although it was primarily a cafe, there was also a shop at the front of the building where coffee beans were sold and ground. The aroma from this was unique and would spread itself wide.

Today, coffee seems to be a very popular drink but during my childhood days, tea was the main beverage of choice. I didn't know anyone who drank coffee except for my mother, and hers came in liquid form in a bottle labelled 'Camp Coffee'. Made from a mixture of coffee, chicory, water and sugar, this is still available today and is apparently popular for making coffee cake. The label on the bottle showed a kilted Gordon Highlander seated on a chest, with a Sikh soldier standing beside him, bearing a tray with a water jug and a bottle of Camp Coffee on top. Today's more politically correct version has the two men seated side-by-side enjoying cups of the coffee together.

Venturing across the river to explore the southern regions of the town, it was always exciting to see a steam train crossing over one of the two bridges that stretched above the High Street junction. Who could have failed to be impressed by the site of such mighty beasts as they sped along pulling strings of coaches behind them? The downside was that if the fuel wasn't burning efficiently, then the engines would emit dense clouds of sour-smelling, acrid black smoke through their chimneys; leaving sooty deposits on everything and everyone they passed.

I would have the opportunity to observe these beautiful giants much more closely whenever I accompanied Granny and her sister to Milverton Cemetery. Both widowed, they never seemed to be in any great hurry, and would always stop when we reached the engine turntable at the corner of Rugby Road and Old Milverton Road, and wait patiently while I watched the engines being turned through 180 degrees to face back in the direction from which they had just come.

Before the clean air act of 1956, most factories were coal-fired, so the steam trains were not solely responsible for the clouds of dirty, smelly smoke that rose up to pollute the atmosphere above the town. Taking into account, also, that few domestic properties of the time were centrally heated, with most people using coal fires to heat their homes, and it is easy to imagine that during the winter months, our lovely Spa could be a very smelly place indeed. The Act required that only clean fuels such as coke, gas and electricity should be used; the powers-that-be seemingly unaware, or perhaps simply choosing to ignore, that 'dirty' coal had to be used in order to produce these 'clean' fuels.

As summer gave way to the chill of autumn, Pat & I would often be sent to the gas works on Saturday mornings, to buy coke for the fire. This was what remained of the coal once the gas had been extracted from it, and was used to supplement the family's coal supply, being much cheaper. Without doubt the works were the pongiest place in town and they were certainly not a place to linger, nevertheless most Saturdays would see little processions of people making their way along Tachbrook Road towards the canal bridge and the gas works, pushing a variety of old prams, pushchairs and handmade go-carts before them.

For Pat & me the journey there was easy enough as it was mainly downhill and we were pushing empty, but coming back was a different matter and it would take both of us to push our laden pram. Our reward would be sixpence each to go to the Saturday morning pictures at the Clifton Cinema. If we were lucky, we might even be given an extra penny or two to buy an apple or a few peanuts from the greengrocer's shop we passed on the way.

Chapter Six
Cream Skirts and Coal Dust

Taking me beneath the arms, my father swooped me high up into the air before carefully bringing me down again to sit atop the plump feather cushion placed ready in the carrier of his delivery-boys bike. Looking back now, the bike seems a strange choice of conveyance for a man who had already passed the midpoint of his forties and was heading towards his half century, but it seems that the bike was a bit of a relic dating back to the days when he sold newspapers in his home village of Cubbington, where, my mother told me, he was the only person licensed to sell the News of the World!

Whatever the reason for having the bike, Dad found it the perfect vehicle for carrying his youngest daughter whenever he took her with him to the allotment, or up into the hills above the town to watch the dirt-track racing. There, we would sit on the grassy bank surrounding the oval track and watch as the young riders raced round and round, each jostling for lead position as they approached the bends. Sometimes they would misjudge things and wheels would touch, sending both bikes and riders crashing to the ground in a flurry of arms and legs and bicycle parts. *

Up in the hills we were surrounded by wild flowers. I was too young then to know the names of them but almost certainly there would have been buttercups and cow parsley; and those grasses with sticky, dart-like seed heads that children love to pick, with the sole intention of sneakily aiming them at the back of some other unsuspecting child.

Perhaps it was the brilliance of the colour that attracted me and lodged it so firmly in my mind, for the one flower I do remember clearly is the wild red poppy that grew in the field above the hollow. Today, the poppy has become the symbol of remembrance for those who have fought and died in battle but, for me, it is also a reminder of those long-ago days of carefree childhood and leisurely summer days spent with my dad.

The allotment was accessed from Northumberland Road; a wide, grass-verged avenue lined with horse chestnut trees, and home to some of the most expensive post-Edwardian houses in town. It was, my mother said, 'Yer Uncle Tom's allotment' but as he was busy doing his bit for King and Country, Dad had taken over working the plot in his absence. Arran Pilot, Scarlet Emperor, Kelvedon Wonder, Greyhound; these are just some of the names I remember from the allotment days. Those who grow vegetables will almost certainly recognise them, but for those who don't...

Arran Pilot is a first early potato which was introduced in 1930. White fleshed with a good flavour, it is resistant to scab and is a heavy cropper.

Scarlet Emperor is a variety of runner bean that dates way back to 1633. Growing to around 6ft tall it has brilliant scarlet flowers and produces long straight beans with a sweet flavour.

Kelvedon Wonder is a short variety of pea introduced in 1925 by Kings, the Kelvedon seed growers. Reaching only to about 45 cms tall, it is suitable for growing in containers. A heavy cropper, it produces long pods each containing six – eight sweet tasting peas.

Greyhound is a pointy variety of cabbage, fast growing – as its name might suggest – and sweet-hearted.

I loved those visits to the allotments where Dad showed me how to sow peas and beans and I learned how to chit potatoes, or simply sat in the warm sunshine and watched the bees and hoverflies visiting the bush that guarded the gate. It was always so peaceful there, the quietness only broken by the sounds of other gardeners working on neighbouring plots, or by the distant drone of men's voices engaged in conversation as they greeted each other or discussed the merits of this variety or that.

Spring turned into summer, and summer into autumn, and then at 11 o'clock on the morning of, Sunday the 11th of November, I found myself perched on my father's shoulders as we joined the huge crowd gathered together opposite the Cenotaph. Suddenly, everyone fell silent and there was a strange stillness in the air. Here and there a tear trickled down a cheek but not a sound could be heard. I, too, stayed silent, the solemnity of those around us enough to keep me quiet, although I was far too young to understand the significance of the occasion. A gun fired, the deafening noise of the explosion magnified as it bounced off the surrounding walls, and instantly the air was filled with birds taking fright from the nearby trees...

Every now and again Dad and I would take the bus on a Sunday afternoon and travel to his home village of Cubbington to visit those of his family who still resided there. His sister, Emma, lived with her husband in an old cottage on the main street. In order to reach it, we had to negotiate a long flight of steps which ran straight up through the pretty gardens fronting the row of cottages. There was an old lilac tree growing by the front door and if this was in flower, then we would always be given a large bunch to take home to Mom. As I recall, the house had just two rooms on the ground floor; the parlour, which seemed to be rarely used and was always kept very neat and tidy, and the cosy kitchen where the family did their day-to-day living.

Uncle Alf had one hand missing and, in its place, he wore a metal hook. As a small child I always found this quite frightening and I never really felt at ease with him, although he was always very kind to me. Whenever we visited, he would take me to see his pigs which were kept in a sty at the back of the cottages. They would greet us noisily and Alf would bend over the wall to scratch their backs, talking to them as if they were children, and then inviting me to do the same. Little did I know that at some time in the future they would almost certainly be appearing on his dinner plate! Meantime Aunt Em would be bustling about in the kitchen preparing tea for us. This would be a simple salad of lettuce and tomatoes, and there was always a large jug containing sticks of crisp green celery.

Before making our way back to Leamington, we would call to see Dad's older brother, Harry, and his wife Flo, who lived on the main road. With only two years between the two men, they were very close. Had been close enough, indeed, to once join each other in a bit of childhood mischief by damaging a newly laid drain. Although only eight and ten years old at the time, they were taken before the local magistrates, where they burst into tears as their mother testified that they had admitted the offence, and said that she had punished them both by giving them a good thrashing and sending them to bed. Mr Pritchard for the Parish Council, said they had been reluctant to take action but felt obliged to do so as there had been so much damage of late. The boys were discharged with a caution and, as far as I know, they never offended again.

If Auntie Beat had already had her own children at the time, then she might have thought twice about the cream pleated skirts and the white gipsy blouses she made for Pat and me one summer. Worn with red blazers they looked very smart but were completely impractical for two active little girls; this being so, they were kept for church or for those other occasions when my mother considered that only Sunday Best would do. Thus, it was, that after lunch one day, our hair was combed, our faces scrubbed clean, and we were put into our smart outfits ready to go visiting.

It was then that Mom made her mistake; giving in to our pestering, and on condition that we didn't get ourselves dirty, she allowed us to wait outside in the street whilst she got herself ready. Oh, how she must later have regretted that decision!

At first, we kept ourselves quietly amused by studying the toys in Mr Harrison's shop window but when our interest in this was exhausted, we turned away in search of something else to do. At that moment a coal lorry turned in at the end of the street and pulled up outside one of the houses. Moments later the door at the passenger side opened and out stepped our very own Dad.

Well, it wasn't often that we got the opportunity to see our dad at work, so off we went, haring down the street towards him as quick as our young legs would carry us; however, mindful of Mom's warning, we stopped short of throwing ourselves upon him and, instead, stood to one side and watched with interest as he hauled himself up onto the lorry and began manhandling the heavy sacks towards the edge. This task completed, he jumped back down onto the pavement and, pressing his back up against the side of the lorry, reached a hand up over his head to grip one of the sacks by its thick rope handle., then bending forward under the weight of his load, he disappeared into the darkened interior of the house at a laboured half trot, his workmate hot on his heels.

Craning our necks forward, we peered into the gloom and watched anxiously until we saw him coming back towards us, the now empty sack clutched tightly beneath an arm. This, he threw down onto the pavement with a gentle thud, causing little puffs of black dust to rise into the air, scenting it with coal. Having repeated their journey several times, the two men stopped to count the empty sacks, checking that they had delivered the correct amount, before throwing them up onto the back of the lorry and securing the sideboards back in place.

Now Dad opened the passenger door but instead of climbing in as we expected, he turned and taking us beneath the armpits, lifted us up, one-by-one, onto the seat. Before we had time to take in what was happening, he and the driver had settled themselves on either side of us and we were moving off, away up the street.

Well now, didn't we think we were grand, sitting there looking down at the people on the pavement and waving importantly to our friends as we passed by. Up the street we went, made a right turn at the top, then along to the next corner and turned right again. All too soon we were turning back into our own street and pulling up outside the door of our house. Dad lifted us down onto the pavement and then with a cheerful wave of his hand he was gone – leaving us to face Mom's wrath and explain our coal-blackened state!

(*BEFORE THE WAR, motorbikes were used for dirt track racing but I am writing now of a time when petrol was still being rationed for the leisure user; a situation that continued until 1950 when petrol rationing finally came to an end. It was, however, briefly reintroduced during the Suez crisis in 1956.)

Chapter Seven
Shopping with Mom

We had just reached the sweet counter in Peacock's Bazaar when Mom bumped into an old friend. Now, there was nothing my mother liked better than a good old gossip and soon the two women were well away. For a time, I waited patiently but when you are still only knee-high to a grasshopper, grown-up talk can be awfully boring, and soon my attention had wandered to the sweet display. I eyed up the prettily coloured candies; they did look good ...and I did like sweeties. I looked up at Mom. She was in full flow now, too busy laughing and talking to take notice of me. I looked back at the sweeties longingly and then, overcome by temptation, I stood on tiptoe and slowly reached up a hand until it found one of the sweets... It did taste good, but to this day I still feel the guilt and shame of what I did.

The families living in the backstreets often lived in very crowded conditions, some in back-to-back houses, or in small cottages with only one room up and one room down, whilst others rented just a single room, sharing the kitchen and the lavatory with the other tenants. Lack of storage space and difficulty keeping food fresh, meant that shopping had to be done on a daily basis and, with the first supermarket still a decade or more away, this could be a very time-consuming business as it meant visiting any number of small individual shops.

At that time The Parade and the streets running off it, were home to a huge number of stores selling just about anything a person might need or want; A piano? Certainly Madam, try Dale Forty on the Parade. Or you might be looking for a snake, in which case you would be sure to find one at Frank's Pet Store in Regent Street. Butchers? Bakers? Well, yer pays yer money and yer takes yer choice.

You would think that with so many stores to choose from, Mom would simply select one of each to provide for her needs, but you would be wrong. She would go to one grocer for this and another for that, perhaps even a third for something else. And at each store we would have to queue and wait to be served by one of the white-coated assistants who inhabited the space behind the counter, for customers didn't select their own purchases as we do today. Indeed, they were actively discouraged from doing so by the DO NOT TOUCH notices dotted about the stores.

Mom did her main shopping at the Co-op in Lansdowne Street. Here, each customer was given a number which they quoted every time they made a purchase. Using this information, once a year the total amount that each customer had spent would be calculated and a cash dividend (the divi) would be awarded accordingly. You could say that it was the forerunner of today's points card schemes.

From time to time, we would go to Woolworths to buy half a pound of cheap broken biscuits for a treat. In those days the biscuits were sold loose from large cube-shaped boxes arranged over the top of the counter. You could buy a selection according to your likes and dislikes, or settle for a half pound of one variety only. Buying broken biscuits was a bit like getting a Lucky Bag, and there was always a pleasant tickle of anticipation since we didn't know what we were getting until the bag was opened.

Woolworth's also had a big island sweet counter where the colourful candies were displayed in glass cases set around the edge. Whenever we had a few pennies to spend, then we might well be found here, slowly walking around the island eyeing up all those tempting goodies in a torment of indecision. Would it be 2oz of dolly mixtures? Or maybe 2oz of liquorice comfits or jelly babies? Even, perhaps, a stick of golden barley sugar? As often as not we would settle for 2oz of lemonade crystals – a powdery substance coloured yellow, and flavoured with lemon. Eating this was quite a messy business as it would entail dampening a forefinger by licking it, then plunging the wet digit into the powder, withdrawing it and sucking off the crystals, repeating the whole process again and again, until we were just left with a rather soggy paper bag with a scattering of crystals still adhering to the inside. Waste not, want not; so, we would turn the bag inside out and greedily lick off every remaining remnant of the sharp yellow powder. Inevitably, we ended up with bright yellow tongues and bright yellow fingers – then we would argue over whose was the yellowest!

You could have searched every single nook and cranny of every greengrocer or grocer in town, and almost certainly you would not have found a single mango, aubergine or pepper; as for coleslaw, pasta and yoghurt...what they? It would be many years before refrigeration and transport had advanced to a level which allowed these exotic foodstuffs to become an everyday part of the British housewife's shopping basket. The only frozen foods I can remember from my childhood days were the ice lollies and ice creams we were allowed as an occasional summer treat.

Clearly the technology was there or we wouldn't have enjoyed these little luxuries, but perhaps the War and its aftermath had prevented the full development of the technology, or it may simply have been that fridges and freezers were not seen as commercially viable propositions at a time when so many of the poorly-paid working classes were struggling simply to keep body and soul together. In any case, at that time many homes were still without electricity and even the street lamps might still be gas lit.

Fish, meat, and cheese, together with other such perishable foods, were displayed and sold from cold marble slabs. Since these foods had a very short shelf life, the shopkeeper would stock only those that he knew he could sell quickly, thus the range of foods available was very limited. Then too, many foods were subject to rationing during the War and this continued for some years afterwards, so that no matter how well off a person might be, they could (in theory!) only purchase the amounts allowed under the rationing system.

No housewife would go shopping without a spacious bag or shopping basket on her arm. You might, if you were persuasive enough, talk a grocer into providing a cardboard box for your purchases, but as these were used for packing the orders of his delivery customers, he regarded them as gold-dust and would be reluctant to part with one unless you were a very good customer indeed.

If your bag wasn't roomy enough to take all of your purchases, you could buy a carrier bag for a few pennies. With the plastic carrier bag not yet invented, these were made from strong brown paper and would have handles made from several layers of the same paper folded together or, alternatively, from strong white string; however, the bag would not take a great deal of weight and it was not unusual to suddenly find your shopping scattered around your feet!

Old habits die hard and in the early days of the NHS, my parents still preferred to use old-fashioned remedies to cure us of our ailments. Mom would dose us up with daily spoonsful of malt and cod liver oil in order to keep our bones strong and to help ward off those winter colds. I thought it was quite revolting and was perfectly happy to miss mine if Mom forgot to give it, but not so Pat, who loved it and would sometimes sneak an extra spoonful when Mom wasn't around. If I thought the malt and cod liver oil was revolting, then the sulphur tablets she gave me to 'clean my blood', were ten times worse. They were just vile; but they seem to have worked because the boils did clear up and I don't ever recall having any since.

71

When I woke up with earache one night, my father brought me downstairs to the fire and then set about warming up a bottle of olive oil. Once he considered that the right temperature had been reached, he poured a little onto some cotton wool and gently placed it into my throbbing ear. Whether it was the soothing action of the warm oil coupled with the heat from the fire that did the trick, or simply the comfort of being nursed on my Daddy's knee, I couldn't say. At any rate, the next thing I knew it was morning and I was back in my cot again. Not only did I have frequent earaches but I also seemed rather prone to nosebleeds. The cure for these was simple and cost nothing at all, as it simply meant having a bunch of cold keys dropped down the back of my dress!

My Mother used to take 'Carter's Little Liver Pills'. Resembling little black pearls, they came packed in dainty drum-shaped boxes and seem to have been promoted as something of a cure-all. I have no idea why Mom took them. We weren't encouraged to ask questions and simply accepted that things were the way they were.

We got all our medicinal needs from Davis the Chemist, in Warwick Street; an old-fashioned, double-fronted shop with huge, brightly coloured, apothecaries' bottles displayed in the windows. The interior was fitted out with wood panelling and shelves in deep warm shades of mahogany, while rows of neat drawers ranged along the wall behind the counter. These were labelled with gold lettering edged in black and looked very smart. There was a welcoming cosiness about the shop and although I didn't much care for the medicines we bought, I did quite enjoy our visits there.

From time to time, Mom would decide to do some knitting and an amount of wool would be purchased. In those days it came in loose skeins which had to be wound into balls before knitting could begin. If only one person was available to do this, then two dining chairs would be used, placed together back-to-back. The loop of wool would then be placed over these and the chairs pulled apart to make the yarn taut, then it could easily be wound into a neat ball. If two people were sharing the job, then one person would slip their hands through the loop, palms together and thumbs raised at right angles so that the yarn sat just in front of them, the hands would then be pulled apart until the wool was held taut and the second person could then commence winding.

Strangely, although I clearly remember the wool winding, I don't ever remember Mom completing any garment during those childhood years. Now, this may be simply down to a gap in my memory, but there are two other possible explanations; the first is that once the initial enthusiasm had worn off, she simply lost interest. The other, and most likely, was financial. Mindful that many people could not afford to purchase all of the yarn for a garment in one go, most wool shops ran a lay-by system, allowing customers to choose their yarn at the start of a project, but just to purchase a skein or two at a time, with the rest of the yarn put to one side for her. Usually, a six-week time limit was observed after which any wool not purchased would be put back on the shelves. I suspect that Mom simply found she couldn't afford to buy those extra balls within the time limit.

She was also able to crochet and attempted to teach me a number of times, but it all seemed very complicated and I was never able to follow her instructions. Embroidery appeared to be her favourite needlecraft and she worked a number of items for the house, most of which seemed to feature wide-skirted crinoline ladies standing amidst an array of colourful garden flowers. She told me that as a teenage pupil in her last year at St Peter's School, instead of lessons, she had to embroider lingerie and table linen for Woodward's store on the Parade, so maybe that is where her embroidery skills were nurtured.

If all that queuing and going from store-to-store made shopping a lengthy business, then my mother's love of a good gossip made it even more so, and sometimes it appeared to me that Mom must know every woman in town, for we never seemed to go far before encountering an Alice or a Gladys, of her acquaintance. Almost always she would stop for a quick chat, but gossiping was what she enjoyed best and her 'quick chats' never were. The curious thing was that she seemed completely unaware of her own loquaciousness, and if she spotted someone and hadn't the time to stop and talk that day, or simply didn't want to, then she would turn to me and say, "Oh, there's so-and-so. Don't let 'er see us or we'll never get away from 'er," apparently quite unaware that people might be saying the same thing about her!

Pat was a bit of a tomboy and would sometimes get herself into little scrapes. I remember standing next to my mother one day as she laughingly regaled an acquaintance with the story of Pat's latest mischievous exploit. As she finished, she glanced down at me then, jerking her thumb in my direction, she gave a big sigh and said "Not like thisen; always got 'er bloody 'ead stuck in a book, she 'as". "Not like thisen" was a phrase I heard often, usually accompanied by some negative observation about me, but on this occasion, there was truth in what she said.

Looking back from this distance, I can see that I was probably quite an inquisitive child, and one which my poor mother was simply ill-equipped to deal with. Even as I write this, I can hear her exasperated voice exclaiming: "Oh, why can't you be like yer sister and go out to play!" The answer to that, of course, is that I was not like my sister, and she was not like me. We were as different as chalk and cheese; she, extrovert and making friends easily, whilst I was introvert and inclined to be shy and timid. She spent most of her free time out & about, and enjoyed rough games of football with the boys; I spent much of my time in the house 'helping' Mom; reading, or playing games of schools or libraries with my dolls, but in spite of our differing personalities, we got on well together and were always good friends.

During my childhood years the town centre was a vast Aladdin's Cave of shops offering just about anything a person might need or want. Some stores, such as Burgis & Colbourne, were huge, reaching right through from The Parade to Bedford Street and stretching upwards some three of four storeys high, whilst others were no bigger than the average front room.

Those being the days before the first supermarkets appeared in town, the streets were well peppered with small food stores to cater for our needs. Of these, the bakers and greengrocers were mainly independent family-run businesses, but many of the grocery shops were part of national chains that could also be found in other big towns.

Dried fruits, glace cherries and such like, would be delivered to the shops packed loose into sacks and boxes, and would then be weighed and put into paper bags by the grocers themselves, ready for sale. Similarly, if a shop also sold provisions, then butter and lard might reach them in giant blocks that needed to be cut into half-pound chunks, before being securely wrapped in greaseproof paper to be sold on.

Large, heavy and drum-shaped, cheeses came covered in a thick crust which grew naturally on them as they matured, and were cut into pieces using a sharp cheese wire. Some people might demand a taste before they purchased as the flavour varied according to maturity. There were, in any case, few varieties available and -- in my opinion – none of them tasted very nice.

Many working-class families shopped for clothes from mail-order catalogues, but there were plenty of clothes shops scattered throughout the town centre for those who wanted more choice. Many of them were small independent businesses but some of the bigger stores also had clothes departments - and there was always good old Marks & Sparks.

At that time Leamington seemed to be well known for the large number of shoe shops to be found in the town, with styles and prices on offer to suit all. If your pockets were very deep, then you might have bought your footwear from Melville's in Victoria Terrace, who described themselves as FOOTWEAR SPECIALISTS. However, Freeman, Hardy and Willis must have been very popular because they had three branches in Leamington, in addition to one in neighbouring Stratford; but, with some twenty stores available in the town, there were shops to suit all pockets, even for those of us who had to settle for second-hand.

One of the most unusual shops was the Chain Library at 65 The Parade. Dating back to medieval times when books were extremely expensive, chain libraries fastened the books to the shelves by a length of chain just long enough to allow them to be removed for reading, but preventing them from being taken away. There are few such libraries left today, with the biggest one in the world being found at Hereford Cathedral.

At that time also, there were still a small number of blacksmiths & farriers in the town, but I was only familiar with the one in Swan Street, this being close to Granny's cottage. If a horse had been visiting then it might well have left a steaming visiting card behind. The gardeners in the area looked upon this as caviar for their gardens and allotments, and were always very willing to remove it from the streets. I remember one afternoon when Uncle George, having come across one such steaming pile whilst cycling home, came dashing into the yard as though the Devil himself was at his heels, quickly grabbed himself a bucket and shovel and then hot-footed it back out again, determined to claim his prize before anyone else could get to it.

Woolworths seemed to sell a little bit of everything; food, clothes, stationery... Most teenage school children carried penknives in their pencil cases back then, and mine was a pretty little turquoise affair that came from our local branch, along with my colouring pencils. These were double ended with a different colour at each end. The knives were used primarily for sharpening pencils and I don't ever recall any child using a knife to stab other children. Indeed, I don't think it even occurred to anyone to do so.

My sister, Rene, used to buy hat shapes which were made of some type of stiffened canvas. These she covered with fabric and decorated with flowers etc. My mother would buy herself a pot of Pond's Coldcream as an occasional treat and when I was old enough, I bought my first ever lipstick from there.

At Christmas, one or two counters would be piled high with all things needed for the festive season and it was from here that we bought our own decorations and cards.

Baubles, I recall, were made from very thin glass and were extremely fragile, so great care was needed when handling them for should one be careless enough to break one, it would shatter into dozens of tiny sharp pieces.

When springtime came round, the shop would look to the needs of local gardeners by offering a small selection of bare-root shrubs and perennials. What they were selling at any one time was often mirrored by what one saw growing in the gardens of the new estates. Forsythia and ribes sanguineum seemed to be very popular choices, along with Ice plant (sedum spectabile) and London's pride (saxifrage). Plastic plant pots were not invented until the sixties or seventies, and plug plants much later than that. Both were inventions that led on to the huge garden centres we know today.

In addition to the shops there were a handful of banks in the town, most of which were housed in elegant and suitably important-looking buildings on The Parade, but since most people were paid in cash on Friday afternoons, relatively few had use of them at that time.

In any case, one couldn't just walk into a bank and open an account. No. A person had to apply and to back up the application with references from suitably qualified persons. Once approved, a cheque book was issued and that was that.

The problem was that many businesses would not accept payment by cheque for fear that it might bounce and they would lose their money. To get round this obstacle, one bank started issuing bank guarantee cards in 1965 and others soon followed. This meant that cheques could then be accepted, with the business owner safe in the knowledge that the bank would guarantee payment. The first ATMs appeared on our streets in the 1980's and in 1987, Barclays introduced the first debit cards. Employers started to pay wages into bank accounts and before long cash-in-hand had disappeared and whatever their status, everyone was banking.

Peacock's Bazaar (also known as Peacock's Stores) opened in Lower Bedford Street in December 1936, flanked on one side by Leamington Tennis Club and by A H Hayes (furnishers) on the other. I have only vague memories of shopping there with my mother but these tell me that the interior was very similar to Woolworth's. The shop was later taken over by Hayes, doubling the floor space of the latter and apparently making it the biggest furniture store in the Midlands outside of Birmingham.

Unfortunately, the newly enlarged store would not be there for long as a fire broke out in the store during the early hours of a May morning in 1951. Attended by 75 firemen and 17 major pumps, it was said to be Leamington's biggest fire. Reports say that two firemen were cut off by the flames for a short time, whilst an assistant arriving for work was so shocked that she had to be taken to the Warneford Hospital for treatment.

In 1953, A H Hayes are shown to be occupying premises in Regent Street but by 1959, they had moved into a new building in Upper Bedford Street which was previously the site of the Scala Cinema. Meanwhile, the site of the fire became a not very attractive, but useful car park , and still performs that role today.

Chapter Eight
Books

Mom was busy ironing with the heavy flat irons she always used in the days before we had electricity. The irons were heated by the fire or on the hob of the cooker and could get very hot indeed, so great care was needed to get the temperature just right. On that particular day she had just started to iron Dad's Sunday-best shirt when the doorbell rang. "Who's that now?" she said with a sigh, standing the iron up on its end and going to see who was there. It was a salesman selling children's books and normally she would have said a polite "No thank you", and closed the door again, but for some reason, on that day, she seemed to be a long time listening to his patter. Having nothing better to do, I decided that I would make myself useful and carry on with the ironing in her stead. True, I had never done any ironing before, but I had watched Mom many times - and how difficult could it be?

Being very careful not to burn myself, I lifted the iron and began to move it across the back of the shirt; however, I had barely started when my mother called me to the door. "What d'you think of these books?" she asked, as the salesman showed me one of the heavy green volumes. Well, I thought they were wonderful, of course, and was soon totally absorbed in what the man was saying - that is, until the smell of scorching fabric reached our nostrils! With an alarmed gasp, Mom rushed back into the room and found the iron just where I had left it – sitting slap bang in the middle of the shirt! In spite of this, she still bought the books, much to my delight.

They were a set of four, covered in a dark green leather-look material and with the words 'The World of Children' embossed in large gold lettering on the spine and across the front cover. They must have cost a small fortune and how she paid for them I can't think, but there was surely never a set of books so well-thumbed as these.

As children, we had very few books. There were those that Pat received from Sunday School, of course, and possibly one or two others given as presents, but the book I remember best was a beautifully illustrated volume of nursery rhymes, its pages filled with the well-known nonsense poems that have delighted children for generations past.

Goosey, Goosey Gander; Humpty Dumpty; Mary, Mary, quite contrary... all were to be found there, but were they really just bits of nonsense? For delve a little deeper into the origins of these little verses and hidden within the lines, you may find tales of persecution, murder, torture and sex.

Goosey, Goosey, Gander

Goosey, Goosey Gander
Where shall I wander?
Upstairs and downstairs
And in my lady's chamber,

There I met an old man
Who wouldn't say his prayers
So, I took him by the left leg
And threw him down the stairs.

Goosey, Goosey Gander, for instance, is said to hark back to the days of the English Civil War and a time when practicing Catholicism was still illegal. Goose is said to be a 16th century term for a prostitute, but it is commonly suggested that in this poem, the word alludes to Cromwell's troops, who are said to have marched in goose-step fashion. They would search the houses of families suspected of allowing the Catholic Mass to be held within their walls, hence: they wandered 'upstairs and downstairs' and even in the lady's bedroom! Here, they 'met an old man who wouldn't say his prayers'. In this instance, 'old man' is a euphemism for a Catholic priest, who would always say his prayers in Latin. That being so, he would either refuse to recite the prayers written in English in the Protestant Prayer Book, or simply would not know them. Whatever the reason, if he did not say the Protestant prayers it was assumed that he was a Catholic, that is to say, 'a left leg` and he would be put to death.

(Many old houses have 'Priest's Holes' – hidden spaces within the house where priests could secrete themselves until the searchers had left))

Humpty Dumpty

Humpty Dumpty sat on a wall,
Humpty Dumpty had a great fall.
All the Kings horses and all the Kings Men
Couldn't put Humpty together again.

Humpty Dumpty is thought to be the pet name for an enormous cannon used by the Royalist troops to defend the walled city of Colchester during The English Civil War. When a shot from a Parliamentarian cannon damaged the wall beneath Humpty, the cannon fell down and broke into so many pieces that the King's troops were unable to repair it and put back together again.

Mary, Mary, Quite Contrary

Mary, Mary, quite contrary,
How does your garden grow?
With silver bells and cockle shells
And pretty maids all in a row.

This rhyme is said to refer to Mary I, daughter of Henry VIII and Catherine of Aragon and a half-sister to Edward VI. It is suggested that the word 'garden' represents the graveyards where those she executed were buried; whilst 'silver bells and cockleshells were both instruments of torture, (silver bells being thumbscrews, while cockleshells were used with painful effect on a gentleman's genitalia) and 'the pretty maids all in a row`, were the people awaiting execution by the Halifax Gibbet, which was an early type of guillotine.

The first book I remember having for my very own was a one volume encyclopaedia given to me for Christmas 1954, by my adored Uncle Tom & his equally adored wife, Beatrice. A slim volume, about the size of an average paperback book, and with a plain brown cover, it was quite unprepossessing in appearance but I found it full of interest, and it came into its own when the boys in my geography class were making a 3D model of a local farm, and used the instructions in the book to do so.

The only other book I remember owning during those childhood years was a paperback edition of Jane Eyre which I had requested one Christmas, and which was given to me by my sister, Rene, and her husband. At the age of thirteen, my head was filled with romance, and Jane was my heroine but today, I prefer something a little meatier with Ian Rankin or Peter Robinson fitting the bill nicely

If there were few books at home, there was always reading material to be had elsewhere. During the early school years, our teachers would read to us but as our own skills improved, we would read quietly to ourselves. All these years later, it is difficult to recall what I was reading then, but I do remember Rumpelstiltskin being in one of my school readers, whilst Millie Molly Mandy was a particular favourite of mine; however, by the time we were in our final year at junior school, we had progressed on to Charles Dickens; to David Copperfield and A Christmas Carol.

There was more Dickens at senior school; Dickens, Shakespeare... and poetry; lots of poetry. The Ancient Mariner, Hiawatha, the Lady of Shallot. These are just a small selection of titles I can recall, but most are long forgotten today I'm afraid, except for odd snatches here and there. Poor William Wordsworth; When he wrote his beautiful, emotive sonnet, Westminster Bridge, in 1803, I doubt if he ever envisaged that 150 years on, a class of 11-year-old schoolgirls might be found roughly dissecting his sensitive work, as they struggled to understand the rules and grammar of poetry.

It was Pat who introduced me to the library and it was probably the best present she ever gave me. During my junior school years, I was a regular visitor, making myself comfortable on the floor as I browsed the books, delighting in the adventures of the Famous Five or the goings-on at Malory Towers.

We had libraries at senior school, although this amounted to nothing more than a double-door cupboard at my last one. At the beginning of the Autumn Term, the School Libraries Service would deliver several boxes of books to the school, and then collect them again just before the next holidays. For a time, I was appointed librarian, along with Norma, my fellow pupil and friend. It was part of our duties to ensure that the books were all collected in at the end of the year. One girl was in hospital being treated for polio, so the headmaster sent us to her home in

Lillington to try and retrieve her book; I can't imagine that anyone would bother to do so today.

(During the first half of the 20th century, in the UK alone, there were on average 7,760 cases of paralytic polio each year, with 750 of those ending in death. Then in the 1950s, an American medical researcher, Dr Jonas Salk, developed a vaccine and a vaccination programme began.

Another medical researcher, Dr Albert Sabin later developed an oral vaccine. This started to be used in 1962 and because of its ease of use; it soon became the vaccine of choice. So successful was the vaccination programme, that in 2019 the WHO announced that there were only 94 cases of wild polio in the whole world.)

I was 13 and in the third year at senior school, when I was instructed by our English teacher, Mr Usher, to submit one of my essays for the school magazine. Entitled 'The Circus comes to Town` it covers one of the events in Leamington's annual social calendar and so I have decided to include it here. Older now, and a great deal wiser, I cannot believe that I wrote about the menagerie being 'a joy to animal-loving people' and I am pleased to say that from 2020, the use of wild animals has been banned in travelling circuses. Meanwhile, my apologies to anyone who is upset by what I have written.

***

THE CIRCUS COMES TO TOWN

Posters appeared all over the town, in shop windows, on hoardings, fences and on doors. The circus was coming! When the day of the arrival of the circus came round, crowds of people were at the station cheering. The procession was led by an Indian elephant, on which was seated the trainer. Behind, holding trunk to tail, was a row of elephants each one a little smaller than the one in front. These were followed by the acrobats and other artistes. Men and women dressed as people from the Wild West were riding beautiful, white, glossy horses. These were followed by the Shetland ponies and in the rear, the band. The music was deafening! The blaring of trumpets, the beating of the drums, the clashing of cymbals, the trumpeting of the elephants all mingled together to make the uproar. Children followed the parade through the town to its pitch.

The circus pitch was in Victoria Park, where the school sports are held. The Big Top was decorated with coloured lights which were switched on at night. From the Campion Hills one could pick out the Big Top at night. Brightly coloured flags fluttered in the breeze at the top of poles. The caravans were parked around the Big Top; most of them were painted cream. The menagerie was at the far side of the Big Top.

The queue was lengthening swiftly and greater grew the noise of the crowd. Children screamed with excitement, while their parents talked quietly to each other, making sure they had either their money or their tickets. At last, the pay-box windows opened, the crowd surged forward and children were called by their parents.

Up the steps and into a seat, looking around one could see that the bandstand was above the artistes' entrance. The ring was painted in bright red and cream and sawdust was spread all over. High up above the heads of the crowd, stretched across the ring was a tightrope.

The first artistes on were the clowns, who had the crowd in fits of laughter with their antics, setting a ramshackle car on fire and then trying to put it out with buckets of water, but succeeding only in swilling themselves with water till it was dripping off them. Then followed the horses and ponies, who danced on their hind legs to music. An elephant was brought into the ring and a horse was made to lie down while the elephant stepped over it. Then came the tight-rope walkers who held the whole audience in breathless suspense while they performed their feats. When the lions came on, the clowns were performing acrobatics whilst the cage was set up. Then the lions came through a tunnel and took their places; they jumped through hoops of fire and made a pyramid. After the lions came acrobats, gambolling, turning somersaults, cartwheels and making pyramids. The Wild West act set the children screaming with excitement.

Visiting the menagerie is a joy to animal-loving people. There are porcupines, their spikes sticking out on their backs like needles, a bear who was just waking up, lions, tigers, ponies and horses and elephants and a llama all placed around the walls of the tent, in their cages and stalls. Then, at last, when the first day ended people wended their way home, children laughing and talking and thrilling at the events of the past afternoon.

***

Chapter Nine
The Gardens

I was pushing my brother's pram through the Jephson Gardens late one afternoon, when the hooter sounded signifying that they were about to close. We were close to Willes Road so I made my way towards that entrance, only to find the gates already shut and firmly locked. Turning, I retraced my steps and quickly headed towards the Newbold Terrace gates but, to my consternation, I found that these were also closed and just as firmly locked. Convinced now that we were locked in, I did the only thing an eight-year-old could do in such circumstances - I stood at the gates and howled!

It wasn't long before my knight-in-shining-armour appeared in the guise of a tall young man making his way home from work. He listened to my tearful tale of woe then quickly took charge of the situation. Without any bother he climbed over the railings, and then helped me to climb over in the opposite direction. Satisfied that I was safely back on terra-firma, he took Tom out of the pram and handed him to me, then he picked up the pram as though there was no weight in it at all, and passed that over the railings too. Finally, he put himself back over and with a cheerful wave of the hand, he was gone.

Originally named Newbold Gardens, they were first developed as promenade gardens in 1834 by the land owner, Edward Willes; however, realising that he could not afford the upkeep of them indefinitely, Edward then gave them to the town in 1846. They were renamed Jephson Gardens in tribute to Dr Henry Jephson, to thank him for the enormous part he had played in promoting the town as a Spa, and a Corinthian-style temple containing a statue of the good Doctor, was later erected in his honour.

Another of the town's philanthropists, Dr John Hitchman, provided work for many of the town's poor labourers by employing them to build footpaths and other structures in the Gardens, including the 100-metre lake which, at that time, would have been dug out by hand. Born in Chipping Norton, the Doctor trained as a surgeon's assistant in Banbury before coming to Leamington.

In 1852, he bought 11 acres of land on the outskirts of the town and turned it into an arboretum, planting it with thousands of trees, shrubs and flowering plants. He later bought more land and in 1862 built a hydrotherapy hospital there. Sadly, he died five years later, but the hospital remained open under the guidance of a Board of Trustees until 1883, when it became The Midland Counties Home for Incurables. It was then taken over by the NHS in 1948, finally closing in 1995. Much of the land was sold for housing but one acre of the woodland remains and can be accessed from St Helen's Road. Three years after Dr Hitchman died, his friend, Dr Jephson, set up a fund to raise money for a fountain to be built in his memory, and this can be found at the west end of the Jephson Gardens, close to the entrance gates.

As more land was developed, the Gardens seem to have become a venue for the more genteel sports such as croquet, archery, boating and tennis; the latter was played there from 1878 – 1942, when the courts were removed as part of the wartime 'Dig for Victory' campaign.

By the time I would have been old enough to appreciate them, all sporting activities seem to have ceased, with the exception of the boating and a very neat little putting green situated at the Willes Road end. Fishing was also popular but from the Mill Garden side of the river banks. As children we were taught to be quiet when in the vicinity of any fisherman so that we wouldn't disturb the fish!

If memory serves me right, during those childhood years one had to pay to get into the Gardens, except on Sundays and on Thursday afternoons, which was early closing day in the town. They were beautiful. The jewel in Leamington's crown and a delightful diversion from our shabby back-street home. It goes without saying that the lake with its wonderful fountains and ever-welcoming family of ducks was always very popular with the children, but I was also fascinated by the huge bed of giant rhubarb (Gunnera Manicata) that curved around the eastern end of the lake.

I was also very taken with the elaborate floral clock which was meticulously planted with low-growing sedums in various shades and colours. It took many hours of back-breaking work to plant this, but looked wonderful when completed. Sadly, it was vandalised a number of times and the Council finally decided to remove it.

As I recall, the small beds in The Clock Tower Garden were always planted with roses but there was also a wide border at one side which was planted up with a colourful selection of dahlias each year, a task which I believe was undertaken by the local Dahlia Society.

There were trees which we were allowed to climb on and trees which we seemed instinctively to know were out of bounds. Sometimes we would chase each other along the paths that twisted and turned through the shrubbery at the eastern end of the Gardens, or we would try to work out the time using the sundial in the Rose Walk.

From time-to-time there would be exhibitions in the Gardens and I recall a school visit to see the work of some of the young modernist sculptors including Dame Barbara Hepworth, who was probably one of the best known of her generation.

Following the devastation of The War years, our local Council was anxious to find ways of bringing more visitors to the town, and so it was that in 1951, The Lights of Leamington were born. Running from the end of July until the beginning of October, they proved immensely popular, with visitors numbering in the hundreds of thousands over the years. Being gated, the gardens could easily be isolated from the rest of the town and this made them the ideal venue for the illuminations. Beautiful by day, the lights transformed them into wonderland by night, and some people returned year after year.

I remember seeing illuminated squirrels scampering up tree trunks to disappear into the deep canopy above, and energetic rabbits leaping across the lawn close to Dr Jephson's temple. In the shrubbery at the Willes Road end of the gardens, colour-changing lights illuminated a small waterfall, and throughout the gardens there were lighted mechanical tableaux tucked into the bushes; however, the attractions were not just limited to the lights.

A huge marquee for dancing was erected on the lawn close to the clock tower, and was always very popular. Equally so, was the Beer Tent, situated in the lower gardens beside the river. (I wonder if any over-inebriated person ever fell in!) It was in this garden, too, that The Guinness Clock could be found. A rather mad mechanical creation on loan from the Guinness Company, it was set to perform its routine at regular intervals, with doors opening, roofs lifting and those famous Guinness toucans dancing round a central pole.

An orchestra played from the small island in the lake, performing the popular music of the day to the ever-changing audience of onlookers gathered round its perimeter. There were variety shows in the Pavilion and slender ballet dancers performed elegant routines to the backdrop of the floral clock.

All this for just one shilling, or one shilling and sixpence on Saturdays, when visitors were rewarded with a spectacular firework display for their extra pennies.

Sadly, the time came when the lights were becoming just too expensive to run; much of the equipment was getting worn out and needed replacing; parking was becoming more of a problem with each year; and people who lived nearby were complaining of the late night rowdyism - and so it was that ten years after they first began, The Lights of Leamington came to an end.

If the Jephson Gardens were synonymous with The Lights of Leamington, then The Pump Room Gardens were synonymous with the annual Flower Show. For we children, the first sign that this was imminent and we were about to lose our playground, albeit briefly, was when a group of workmen appeared, and started to construct a rockery by the Meteorological Station which occupied a spot on the grassed area between the bandstand and the main footpath.

Over the next few days, tents and awnings of all shapes and sizes would be erected, the most impressive being an enormous marquee covering the whole of the green opposite to St Peter's Church. The interior of this would be for the eyes of the exhibitors, the judges, and the paying public only, and so a paling fence was erected around the whole of the exterior, creating its own secure little island to guard against sneaky interlopers.

Those who couldn't afford the entrance fees were thrown a few crumbs of comfort on the last afternoon of the show, when the tent flaps were thrown wide open to all, free of charge. This seemed to be the signal for the exhibitors to start dismantling the displays and any person who paused to inspect one, might well have found a bunch of cut flowers being pushed into their hands, water still dripping from the ends of the stalks. Although they were disappearing so quickly, the scent of the flowers lingered on, trapped within the warm confines of that huge canvas. The collective scents of so many blooms massed together was overpowering... intoxicating even, and quite impossible to put into words.

The show was organised by The Royal Leamington Spa Horticultural Society, with the first one taking place in 1949 and the last, some 30 years later. The show very quickly won accolades for its high standards but sadly, in spite of being highly appraised by members of the gardening world, the show eventually had to be brought to an end for financial reasons, but it had provided a great deal of pleasure to many people over the years, not least for one little girl from the backstreets, who proudly bore home those bunches of flowers to her mom.

The gardens were created in 1814 as a private exercise space for those wealthy patrons receiving Spa Water Treatment inside the Pump Room buildings, but as the fashion for taking the waters declined and there were fewer visitors to the town, in 1875 it was decided to open up the gardens to the general public. They have undergone many changes over their 200 + years, with York Bridge being put over the river in 1893, and a new bandstand installed in 1889, but on the whole, there have been few changes during my lifetime. The hedge that marked the eastern boundary was removed many years ago, along with the shrub beds at the corner of Dormer place, and the rose beds that bordered all the footpaths radiating out from the bandstand. A pretty shade of pink, they provided a glorious splash of colour in the gardens throughout the summer months. To my mind, the gardens lost some of their lustre with the removal of the beds and have never seemed quite complete without them.

Although the biggest, the flower show was by no means the only event to take place in the gardens and there would be fetes and fairs taking place throughout the summer months. A Punch and Judy show visited, fencing off an area close to the swimming baths and arranging chairs within it for the comfort of their paying audience. Those of us who couldn't pay for this little luxury, would simply stand outside the paling fence and view the show for free from there.

A frequent visitor to the gardens was Miss Newcombe who would regularly bring down two ponies from the riding stables at Newbold Comyn to offer pony rides to visiting children.

Other frequent visitors were the military bands that entertained us on many weekends during the summer months. There were benches surrounding the bandstand for those who wanted to sit back and listen, but if these were all taken or one just wanted a more comfortable seat, then a deckchair could be hired from the man at the wooden hut on the river bank.

There were drinking fountains in all three riverside gardens; Victoria Park, The Pumproom and The Jephson Gardens. Made of metal, all three were of the same design comprising a supporting column with a bowl on top and a knob at one side to operate it. When this was turned, water would shoot up from a nozzle placed in the middle of the bowl.

Until 1875, Leamington's domestic water supply came from the polluted River Leam and Dr John Hitchman had long worked to try and find an alternative source of clean water but without success. It took Alderman Henry Bright and his supporters to finally achieve this, despite much opposition from those who accused him of trying to ruin the town's reputation as a Spa. An obelisk was erected at the Parade end of Holly Walk in honour of Henry Bright and his achievement. This was no ordinary obelisk however, as it was connected to the new water supply and, when I was a child, it was possible to get a drink from there using the metal cup securely chained to it.

In 1861, Blondin,** the world famous tightrope walker, had walked his tightrope across the Pump Room Gardens in front of a crowd of some 7,000 people, but the most unusual event I can recall was the mile-long swimming race in the river Leam, which took place in 1953 and was organised by the Lucas Sports Club of Birmingham. In my memory this started at the York Bridge and ended at the Princes Drive weir.

Now, today, you wouldn't even want to put a big toe in the river, but back in the day, the water was crystal clear and, as a young teenager, I spent many happy hours splashing around in its upper reaches at White Bridge, totally oblivious to the cows that came down to the river to drink nearby - and lift their tails to do what comes naturally, should the urge take them! *

(*SINCE I WROTE THIS, Severn Trent have announced plans to explore the possibility of providing swimming quality water in the area of the river passing through the Pumproom Gardens.

**BLONDIN repeated his walk in 1862 and then returned to the town again in 1873 as part of his farewell tour, this time walking across the lake in the Jephson Gardens.)

Chapter Ten
Playtime

I was playing alone in the street when Mrs Hastings came to her door and called me. "Do you know the vets in Guy's Street?" she enquired, then, having ascertained that I did, she requested that I take her cat there and ask the vet to put it to sleep. I willingly agreed, and the old pet curled up in my arms without protest, making no attempt to escape as I carried it along, chatting away to it as we went. Later, I showed Pat the silver sixpence Mrs Hastings had given me and she was horrified by what I had done, asking me if I knew what it meant to put an animal to sleep, then going on to tell me in some detail.

We often ran errands for the neighbours but usually it would be for nothing more serious than posting a letter perhaps, or taking a pop bottle back to the shop. In those days bottles were made of glass and a bottle-deposit was included in the price to encourage people to return them for re-use. As often as not we would be told that we could keep the money, which we might then spend on sweets from the same shop.

One of the more unusual errands I was sent on came shortly before The Coronation in 1953, when the young woman who lived next door handed me a snippet of red fabric, and sent me to Grey's to get a small amount of the same. Unfortunately, they didn't have any of the fabric left, but they did have something similar and I was given a sample to take and see if that would do instead; it would, and Irene was able to carry on dressing the dolls that were to be given as Coronation gifts to the younger girls living in the street.

Quite often Mom would trust me with a very important message, handing me the rent book together with the necessary sum of money, and instructing me to go to Locke & England to pay the rent, but the job I hated most was to be sent to Woolworth's to get a new gas mantle. These fitted over the naked flames of the gas lights and were as fragile as gossamer; My heart would be in my mouth as I carried it home in its little box, hardly daring to breathe for fear that I might break it.

The street was our playground. We didn't have many toys but were adept at keeping ourselves amused with very little, or even nothing at all. There were games of tig or underarm release. In this game any child who was caught by the person who was 'on', would have to stand with arms outstretched until released by another child running beneath one of them. Another version of this had us scrambling through the legs of the 'caught' child.

Kiss chase was always popular with the girls but less so with the boys, who would twist and turn and summon up all the speed they could muster in order to avoid the outstretched arms of the girls. And should one find himself being caught anyway, then the unfortunate boy would twist and turn even more as he tried to escape from being kissed, only to find himself being firmly held by one or more of his laughing friends who, whilst not wanting to be kissed themselves, relished seeing one of their pals suffering that indignity!

There were games of 'What's the time Mr Wolf?' and 'Farmer, Farmer, may we cross your field?` which often had the girls lifting their skirts to see if the requested colour might be found on their underclothing! Other times, we might play hopscotch, chalking a large grid on the pavement; or we might sit in the gutter playing games of marbles or five-stones. A length of old washing line did service as a skipping rope, which was a versatile game as it could be played solo or as a group activity. Mostly, it was played by the girls as the boys considered it a bit cissy and preferred to take themselves off to the Pump Room Gardens for a game of football or cricket, using their jumpers or coats to mark out the goalposts and wickets.

A popular game for all was 'fag cards`. Bearing a picture on one side and an explanatory text on the other, the cards were given away with certain brands of cigarettes. The subjects covered were wide-ranging and could vary from animals and plants, to various modes of transport or famous sportsmen. Some adults would collect them until they had a complete set to frame and hang on the wall. Today, these sets of cards are much sort after and can sell for sizeable sums of money.

Our game had us sitting on the kerb, flicking cards across the pavement in turn. The aim was to cover your opponent's cards and, if successful, they became yours. Some children were guaranteed a supply of cards by cigarette-smoking parents and other family members, but those of us who didn't would scour the pavements and bins for discarded packets, or even approach complete strangers to ask for their cards.

We played a similar game with milk bottle tops. The glass bottles used at that time were wide-necked, with a groove running round the inside into which would sit the cardboard disc used to seal the milk into the bottle. The discs would usually carry the name of the dairy and, as most of us had milk delivered, they were easier to come by than the cigarette cards. Since the tops could have the middles punched out to form a circular hole, they were also ideal for the girls to make big fluffy pom-poms from scraps of coloured wools.

Our mother made us Knitting Nancy's by hammering four tacks into one end of a wooden cotton reel. Together with a hairgrip and a few scraps of wool, we were furnished with all that we needed to make colourful cords. When long enough, these could be sewn into a circular shape to form a mat or even a hat. I'm not sure that we ever did that but making the cords kept us busy for hours on those cold, wet days when we were not inclined to play out.

On such days we might play snakes & ladders, or card games such as snap or pontoon. There were paper games too, with hangman being a favourite. Or we might fold sheets of newspaper and cut shapes out of them, before unfolding them again to reveal rows of snowflakes or dancing figures. I kept a scrapbook filled with pictures of the Royal family, which I cut out from the newspapers and attached to the book's pages with glue made from a mixture of flour and water.

Ball games were enjoyed by boys and girls alike. There was 'Piggy in the Middle`, with the youngest child usually appointed as 'Piggy`; whilst 'Two Balls' was always popular with the girls. This was played by throwing two balls alternatively against a wall, whilst keeping in time to a rhyme:

One, Two, Three, O'Leary
Four, Five, Six, O'Leary
Seven, Eight, Nine, O'Leary
Ten, O'Leary, catch the ball....ie

One, Two, Three, and over
Four, Five, Six and over
Seven, Eight, Nine, and over
Ten and over, catch the ball...ie

One, Two, Three, and under
Four, Five, Six and under
Seven, Eight, Nine, and under,
Ten and under, drop the ball...ie.

Often, we would amuse ourselves by practising our gymnastic abilities, performing handstands and cartwheels, or attempting to do 'the crab` by bending over backwards and using our hands to 'walk' down a convenient wall. I don't think any of us were very successful at this except for our friend, Pat, who lived in a neighbouring street but often came to play in ours. A tall, willowy girl with deep brown eyes and a mass of dark hair, Pat seemed to be blessed with a natural gymnastic ability, and could do 'the crab` with the greatest of ease by simply bending over backwards and placing her hands straight onto the pavement, leaving the rest of us quite green with envy.

There must have been some thirty or forty children and young teenagers living in the street, but not all of them were allowed to play out. Others were allowed to come out and join in our games, but were forbidden to leave the street, and the rest were allowed to roam at will. Pat and I were amongst the latter group, coming and going as we pleased with few restrictions – the feral children of our day. My Mother's only concern was that we didn't do anything to bring the police knocking at the door, and most of the time she hadn't a clue where we were or what we were doing.

In truth, just about the most mischievous thing we ever did was to throw sticks at the horse chestnut trees in the Holly Walk, in an attempt to dislodge the fruits. Sometimes their prickly green overcoats would split open as they hit the ground, casting out the beautiful shiny jewel sealed within, but other times they were not quite ready to give up their treasure, and the cases would simply split into a smile, revealing just a tantalizing glimpse of its mahogany contents.

We spent much of our time in Victoria Park splashing about in the paddling pool or playing on the swings. There were two types of plank swing, one of which, pivoted at both ends, simply moved back and forth getting a little higher with each swing but always remaining horizontal with the ground. The other, much favoured by the older children, was attached by central pivots which gave the seat the freedom to swing higher and higher at each end until it was almost heart-stoppingly vertical. The ambition was always to go 'over the top` but no-one ever could, of course.

The slide was a monster — or so it seemed back then. We would pile onto it a dozen or more at a time and make our way up a ladder bordered by stout handrails, but when we reached the top, there was only a small extension of this to help us make the transition from ladder to slide in safety. The witches' hat was always a favourite, and it was often difficult to find a spare patch of seat to slide one's bottom into, while the swings were always in great demand... but all are long gone now, having fallen victim to the modern health and safety regulations.

From time-to-time, we would hunt for lost tennis balls in amongst the shrubs that surrounded the tennis courts, or we might even stop to watch a game in progress. A favourite pastime for we girls was making daisy chains from the pretty white flowers that grew on the river bank in abundance, or we would lie on our tummies and watch the fish darting in and out of the reeds.

Sometimes we would try our hands at fishing, using nets fashioned from a length of bamboo, a piece of wire and a scrap of old net curtaining. To bring home our catch, we would take with us a jam jar suspended from a handle made of string, but these were never used for the intended purpose because, not surprisingly, we didn't ever catch anything!

Other times, we might stop to watch a game of bowls which might be taking place on the bowling green, but we always stood at the gates, never daring to venture inside. Everything was so pristine and manicured that the very idea of disturbing such perfection felt quite threatening, in the way one might feel when walking into the home of a house-proud woman and be almost afraid to sit down, lest you should disturb the symmetry of the cushions she had arranged with such precision.

Designed by Borough Engineer, William Louis de Normanville, the Park was opened in 1897 to celebrate Queen Victoria's Diamond Jubilee. Much of the land used had been previously leased for some 50 years by two prominent cricketers, George Parr and John Wisden, the latter being of Wisden's Almanac fame. During their lifetimes, the grounds were used for cricket and archery, and a cricket pitch was thus included in de Normanville's design, together with the circular running & cycling track that measures exactly half a mile long.

Throughout the 20th century, the park was used for events that attracted large gatherings of people and it was here that the inter-school sports were held during my early school years. I would like to claim that I was a highly successful competitor, a star of the athletic world, but it wouldn't be true for, sadly, my sporting abilities did not match my enthusiasm and I was forced to be content with just sitting on the side-lines, cheering on my fellow pupils.

Towards the end of October our thoughts would turn to Bonfire Night and so we would set about collecting together the materials to make our Guy. Our parents could usually be relied on to provide old clothes but, if not, then a kindly neighbour might help out instead. With the Clothes sorted there was only one place to go for the stuffing material and so we would make a rare foray into Kenilworth Street and Ballingers' warehouse, * where a polite request for straw usually led to an invitation to come inside and help ourselves.

Lantern Corner was a favourite place to park our guy and way-lay passers-by with polite requests for "A penny for the Guy, please". We were never going to make a fortune but whenever we had enough coins collected, we would take them to a tiny shop in Regent Grove and exchange them for fireworks. Silver Fountains, Golden Rain, Catherine Wheels and Roman Candles were some of our favourites, whilst sparklers were an absolute must. The bonfire was built on waste-land behind the Gleason's house, with Mr Gleason supervising and bringing the evening to a close by treating us to jacket potatoes cooked in its dying embers.

(*BALLENGER'S were plumbers' merchants with warehouses in Kenilworth Street and showrooms in Regent Street.)

Chapter Eleven
Cars, Bicycles and Shanks' Pony

He came running into the street, eyes alight with excitement. "There's a gold car on the Parade" he shouted, "Come and see."

A GOLD car? WOW!!!

Moments later I was joining the other children tearing along Warwick Street, desperate to reach The Parade before the car was driven off again. We turned the corner and there it was, parked right outside the Tax Office, a magnificent Daimler belonging to Sir Bernard Docker, Managing Director of the Birmingham Small Arms Company (BSA) and Chair of The Daimler Company Ltd. Guarded by a uniformed chauffeur, it did indeed gleam gold in places where other cars simply shone silver, but it just wasn't gold enough to match the picture in my head, and I felt hugely disappointed.

It was a peaceful Sunday afternoon and Park Street was deserted except for Pat and her friend, quietly chatting as they walked along. They had almost reached our house when a man turned his car into the street and pulled up alongside them, then he leaned across the seat, and opening the door, asked if they could direct him to the Regal

Cinema. They could, and with much hand pointing, they did, but he seemed not to understand and suggested that they get into the car and show him, offering them a bag of sweets if they did so. However, mindful of the warnings they had been given, the girls refused, at which point he leaned back in his seat again, fiddled with his trouser fly for a moment, and then revealed his erect penis.

A few moments later the girls burst in through our front door, both talking at once as they attempted to tell my mother what had happened. Once she had calmed them down enough to make sense of what they were saying, she looked at the clock, and then calmly sent them out again to look for our regular beat bobby, saying that he would be in Warwick Street at that time of the day; and sure enough, as they turned the corner, there he was coming along the street towards them.

Seeing the girls come back to the house accompanied by the policeman, Mr Davis left his shop and came over to speak to him. He had gone into the shop to re-dress the window, he explained, when he noticed a car stopped opposite. As we didn't get many cars visiting Park Street, he'd been curious and had watched as the man spoke to the girls, then seeing the alarmed look on their faces, he realised that something was awry, and so he had noted down the car's number as it drove away. Thanks to his diligence, the car was spotted near to Stratford later that afternoon, and just in time it would seem, for we were told later that a young girl was found sitting beside the driver, clutching the bag of sweets.

Very few working-class families could boast a car in the forties and fifties, and those that did were often inclined to treat them as Sunday Best, washing them down in the morning perhaps, and then taking them out for a drive to some beauty spot in the afternoon. Invariably it was the men who did the driving, whilst the women sat in the passenger seat and – dare I say it – instructed them how to!

On week days however, it was the bicycle that ruled the road and when the day's work was done, cyclists numbering in the hundreds could be seen swarming out of local factory gates. Those who didn't have a bike might climb aboard one of the many buses lined up ready to deliver them as close to their homes as the bus routes would allow, but for everyone else it was plain old shanks' pony.

By the time I left school in 1958, the motorised scooter (moped) had become very popular, especially amongst teenage boys. One of the boys I worked with was the proud owner of one such machine, and I was delighted when he offered to give me a lift home one evening. It was icy cold, and unable to afford bus fares every day out of my miserly wages, I had been faced with the prospect of a long, cold, walk home. I had no romantic interest in the boy and he had never shown any in me, so as I settled myself behind him and put my arms about his waist, I was completely unaware that my closeness might be arousing feelings in him that I, in my innocence, knew nothing about.

'We'll be home in no time' I told myself, but to my surprise, instead of taking me home, he headed out into the countryside and pulled off the road into some bushes. There he demanded that I let him 'do it' or he would just leave me there to find my own way back home. Well, I had no idea what IT was but, whatever, I certainly wasn't going to do it with him, so I pushed him away from me and started to walk back towards the road. Perhaps realising that he could be in big trouble if anything happened to me, he followed, apologising profusely, and persuaded me to get back on the moped again. This time he did take me home; nothing more was said about the incident and he never offered me a lift again.

With foreign package holidays still on the distance horizon, the Great British working classes headed for the Great British seaside when holiday time came round. Some would stay in boarding houses which, by many accounts, were often not very pleasant places, with bathrooms being shared with the other guests and the holiday-makers expected to stay out of the houses during the day, but to be back before the landlady locked up in the late evening.

Other holiday makers would hire caravans. These were often very basic affairs offering little more than a bed to sleep on, with toilets and showers being shared with the other holiday makers and housed in unattractive concrete blocks around the site. Often the caravan sites were nothing more than an empty field but others would offer extra facilities such as a shop, and a club house. Holiday parks were a step up, often offering chalets instead of caravans, and providing entertainments including children's clubs so that parents could relax and enjoy their own pursuits.

Many people travelled by train but those with cars would usually opt for making the journey by road; however, cars at that time were not as efficient as today's models and had a tendency to overheat on long summer journeys, and especially so if that journey involved any steep hills. This seemed to be the straw that broke the camel's back for many vehicles and it was not at all unusual to see lines of cars stopped at the side of the road, with steam coming out from beneath the bonnets. Winter brought a different problem as the engines would simply refuse to start on cold, frosty mornings.

For the poverty classes, holidays could be counted in days, if indeed, there were any to be counted at all. For me that meant those days spent in London and Weston-Super-Mare with my Aunt and Uncle, and another seaside trip with them a few years later, this time to Hayling Island. I was probably the ideal companion for them on that day, being still young enough to enjoy making sandcastles with their small daughter but also old enough to keep a watchful eye on her, allowing them to relax a little.

Somewhere along the way my father had started joining a colleague on a retreat held at Offchurch Bury every year. It wasn't quite a holiday and I'm not sure what, if anything, he gained from it, but away he would go leaving my mother to cope alone with anything that happened on the home front. He also went on the annual pub outing to Llandudno, where the men would have lunch at the hotel owned by their hero, Randolph Turpin. Born in Leamington but raised in Warwick, Randolph became World Middleweight boxing champion in 1951, after beating Sugar Ray Robinson.

My sister Rene's husband had been in the Royal Navy serving on board HMS Vanguard. When he discovered that the ship was going to be in Portsmouth for Navy Day one year, he was keen to take his young wife to see it, and had then persuaded my father that the whole family should accompany them on the one-day coach trip. Other than going to Birmingham for Uncle Jim's wedding, this was the only time I can remember the whole family ever going anywhere together.

We had a great day but when coming home again we had just reached the canal bridge in Tachbrook Road when my poor mother, who had been quietly feeling rather unwell for some time, suddenly discovered that she could no longer hold it together and violently deposited the contents of her stomach down the front of her new coat!

The next day the coat was taken to be cleaned, but so familiar was Mom with the dry cleaners, that she simply didn't realise they operated a 'collect by' system, and by the time she had enough money saved to collect it, the coat had been sold on. In a moment of unusual largesse, my father had bought the pale grey coat for Mom from Rene's Mail Order catalogue the previous Christmas, and had barely finished paying for it, so he was furious with my mother for losing it that way.

Chapter Twelve
Christmas

It may have been the year when I was eight; or it may have been the year when I was nine, no matter... It was Christmas Eve and we were curled up close together in the middle of the big bed we shared with our parents when she told me. "There isn't really a Father Christmas, you know; it's our mom who puts the things in our stockings."

If I'd been any way towards falling asleep when she said it, then the shock of her statement would surely have had me instantly wide awake again. No Father Christmas...Mom...? She couldn't possibly be serious... but she assured me that she was.

"Just you stay awake and you'll see for yourself." she added firmly, and then made sure that I did, by giving me a sharp poke whenever she judged that I might be in danger of heading for the Land of Nod. At last, we heard the sound of the stair door opening and soft footsteps on the bare boards.

"Shush!" Pat warned "Close your eyes and pretend to be asleep."

Christmas was a magical time, starting with the placing of a life-sized crib on one of the side-alters at church and, at school, there would always be cards and a calendar to create and take home as gifts for our parents. Every year there would be a Christmas party with the food being donated by our parents and well-wishers. Mrs Rogers would always donate jelly; several pints of it, made in one of the enormous enamel bowls that usually held the batter for the fish.

One year my mother promised a blancmange for the feast but then forgot all about it until I arrived home for lunch on the appointed day. At first there was much huffing and puffing along the lines of "I've got better things to do with my time than to be making blancmanges for your school parties." but then she remembered that it had been snowing heavily that morning and that gave her an idea. She quickly set to work making the milky treat, then poured it into a dish and set forth for the top yard, carefully bearing her offering before her. Once there, she paused for a moment to look around her - and then set the dish down in the deepest pile of snow she could find.

I loved going to the Christmas Bazaar in St Peter's Church Hall and although I only ever had a few pennies to spend, I was kept well entertained by looking at the things for sale or watching people try the various games on offer. The nuns always had a stall selling the embroideries they had worked on throughout the year and, oh! how I coveted the pretty tablecloths they hung from the walls, the better to display them. On another stall, it was the knitted baby booties that took my attention; white, lacy and as light as thistledown, they were so delicate and pretty, and I was totally in awe that anyone could produce something so complicated & dainty. One stall had a jar of colourful sweets on display with a notice inviting us to 'Guess the number of sweets in the jar'. With sweets having still been rationed until April, 1949, I imagine this would have been a very popular prize.

Other games included a 'Guess the weight of the cake' competition and a treasure hunt, but by far the most popular and entertaining game was the Buzz Wire. In this game the player would hold a wooden handle with a hoop of metal attached to one end, and try to pass the hoop over a wire track without touching it, thus causing it to make a buzzing noise. It sounds simple but is actually quite hard to do and most people wouldn't progress very far, but occasionally someone would get a good way along and then everyone would go quiet, holding their breath, and silently willing the player on to the end.

During the day we would practise our Christmas Carols at school, and in the evening, we might pay a visit to the occupants of Lansdowne Circus and treat them to an off-key rendition of Come All Ye Faithful or Silent Night. There was a Carol Service held in church, but it was the Salvation Army Service held outside the Town Hall, that I enjoyed the most.

Window shopping was a favourite pastime in the run up to Christmas, and I could often be found with my nose pressed up against a piece of window glass studying the goodies displayed so temptingly on the other side. One of my favourite shops was Bailey's in Warwick Street, where the window to the left of the door was always given over to the toy display. At the front of the window was a conveyer belt with model cars attached and I would watch in total fascination as the vehicles travelled along in front of me, then disappeared beneath the floorboards out of sight, only to pop up again at the other end of the track moments later.

Christmas Eve was always busy with food to be got and last-minute gifts to be bought and wrapped. My Mother would pay into various Christmas Clubs throughout the year thus ensuring that we had a few extra treats come the big day, but only when she had all the essentials bought would she consider if she could afford to buy anything extra. This would usually mean a last minute trip to Woolworth's, and I can remember being sent there one time to get a pop-up picture book for her brother's small daughter, together with a sheet or two of the colourful wrapping paper which was always stacked high on the counter and sold by the sheet; but at last the shops were closed, the wrapping was done and we could relax and enjoy a simple tea consisting of thick, chunky slices of bread, toasted over the open fire at the end of a long-handled metal toasting fork, and spread with delicious beef dripping.

Putting up the decorations was always an exciting time. We used reels of colourful crepe paper which, when pulled out from the middle, formed twisted streamers to drape across the ceiling. To these we would add large paper balls & bells, paper-chains and bunches of big fat balloons. We made the chains ourselves, using strips of brightly coloured paper sold in little packs especially for that purpose.

Our Christmas tree was artificial and a very modest affair, about two feet high with branches that resembled obese bottle brushes, jutting out at right angles from a centre stem. One by one we would carefully attach the delicate glass baubles that came in brilliant shades of red & green and gold & silver. There were glass birds too, with luxuriantly long tails flowing out behind them and, most important of all, a battered old fairy who came out of hiding each year to sit atop the tree and oversee the celebrations. Finally, we would clip candle holders to the branches and insert twisty red candles into each one.

Mom never had any problems getting us to bed on Christmas Eve, although excitement might keep us awake for a good while after. I always hoped to get a glimpse of Father Christmas but I never did. Strange that he always seemed to know just when I had fallen asleep before paying his annual visit! The contents of our stockings were modest; a tangerine, a few copper coins, and a selection of liquorice shapes; a balloon perhaps, plus just one small toy. I remember one year being given a money box shaped like a rotund red post box – perhaps Mom thought it would encourage me to save the copper coins.

We only ever had one main present from our parents and, since Mom would have bought those through her Christmas Club savings, what we got was very much dictated by what was available at the shop she had been saving with. One year I had a toy telephone – which I was delighted with – and another time I was given a pushchair for my doll. Made of metal and painted blue, it had a very distinctive shape and I have never seen another one like it. The most disappointing present I ever had was the

Compendium of Children's Games I was given one year. Thirteen, going on fourteen, I was fast growing up and had so wanted a fashionable hounds-tooth check skirt, just like the ones worn by the most popular girls in my class. The following year I did get one, but it was far too big for my slender frame and so it was passed on to Pat.

We always had chicken for Christmas dinner. A common, everyday dish now, but in those post-war years it was expensive and considered something of a luxury. It was served with sage and onion stuffing, potatoes - both mashed and roasted - and sprouts, but no pigs-in blankets, cranberry sauce or sweet red cabbage, these being more recent additions to the feast. If the sprouts were bitter, my father would declare that this was because they hadn't been frosted before they were picked, the frost apparently making them sweeter. There was always Christmas pudding to follow. My mother seemed to enjoy this but I don't think anyone else was very keen, finding it too rich and heavy.

On Christmas night we would join some of the aunts and uncles for a party at Granny's house in Lansdowne Road - although it is something of a mystery how we all managed to squeeze into her tiny cottage. Immediately inside the door the spot usually reserved for her china cabinet would now be occupied by a pine Christmas tree, so tall that it almost reached the ceiling. Just like our own tree, the branches would be laden with colourful baubles and delicate glass birds, but added to these would also be bright orange tangerines and rolls of sweets tied on with strong thread. Since Granny's house had electricity, her tree boasted a string of electric lights instead of candles, each bulb being shielded by a trumpet shaped hood decorated with colourful Disney characters. The air inside the room was always heavy with the scent of the citrus fruits mingling with that of the pine tree, and even all these years on, whenever I smell those two scents, I am immediately transported back to childhood and Christmas at Granny's.

The dining table, now fully extended and covered by a crisp white cloth, would almost groan beneath the weight of the food piled upon it. There were jellies and blancmanges, tinned fruits and evaporated milk to pour over them; tinned salmon sandwiches, sausage rolls and pork pies... and just when we were all full to bursting and thought we couldn't possibly eat anything more, in would come the beautiful cake made by Auntie Beat and abundantly decorated with tiny trees and porcelain figures.

Once everyone had eaten their fill, the table would be cleared and put outside into the blue-bricked yard, to make room for some fun & games. We would do the Hokey-Cokey and dance the Conga; and Uncle Tom would always invite me to place my tiny child-sized feet on top of his generous man-sized ones, to waltz me round the floor. We played pass-the-parcel when surely there must have been some cheating going on to be certain that everyone had a prize. One time I was delighted to win a bottle of Amami Wave Lotion and had to be handsomely bribed before I would swap with an aunt for something more suitable. Perhaps I had visions of Shirley Temple Hair!

Part way through the evening, Uncle Tom would put on his record of Jingle Bells and we would all join in, singing at the tops of our voices. Even as the last notes faded away there would be a knock on the door and in would walk Father Christmas himself, carrying a bulging sack on his back. After cheerfully greeting us all, he would set the sack down on the floor and begin to give out the parcels contained within it. One time he lifted me up into his arms and asked for a kiss; I was horrified by this and promptly burst into tears! Playing the part of Father Christmas, poor Uncle Jim must have been quite mortified by my reaction.

One year, Pat and I were given dolls by Uncle Tom and Auntie Beat. Multi-jointed and with go-to-sleep eyes, they were beautifully dressed, right through from the pretty lace-trimmed underwear to their cosy woollen coats and hats. They even had tiny muffs hanging from slender cords around the neck. Auntie, we knew, already possessed several such dolls, which she used to create colourful Easter and Christmas displays in the window of her parents' bakery shop. They were beautiful, the crème-de-le-crème of the doll world as far as we were concerned, and we could often be found with our noses pressed up against the window, gazing wistfully at a blue-eyed blonde swinging above a meadow of artificial grass and flowers, or a brown-eyed brunette frolicking in cotton wool snow. To each be given one of these dolls for our very own was more than we could ever have wished for and we went to bed that night, two very happy little girls.

By the time everyone had opened their parcels, it would be getting late and the grown-ups would begin to wind the evening down. We would play Escalado, backing our horses with farthings or halfpennies, and then Uncle Tom would erect a screen over the fireplace and we would all settle down to watch a silent movie before leaving for home. One year it started to snow just as we were leaving and it seemed like magic!

Another time we encountered a young neighbour when we were making our way home. Filled with Christmas cheer, he lurched drunkenly towards us, arms outstretched in greeting, and I, half asleep in my Daddy's arms, let out a piercing scream and clung to him in terror, quite convinced that this strange man was about to attack us. The young Mr then set about trying to make reparation by reaching out a hand and patting me on the head, which just sent me into a complete panic and made me scream even more!

Chapter Thirteen
Granny Moore

I loved my Granny. She was so quiet and gentle and never raised her voice to us. I liked visiting her in her little cottage where she lived with my sister Rene, who she had cared for since she was five years old. I sometimes stayed there, sleeping with Granny in her big double bed which always seemed to be covered with crisp white cotton sheets. A picture of a handsome stag hung on one wall of the bedroom, almost certainly a print of Landseer's, 'Monarch of the Glen`, whilst on another were two pictures depicting black silhouettes of dancing girls set against a brilliant blue background, all shiny and iridescent. Years later my mother told me that the background was created from butterfly wings, which I thought rather gruesome.

Sometimes I would accompany Granny and my mother when they visited Leamington Cemetery to put flowers on Grandad's grave. In the spring it would always be wallflowers because Granny loved their scent and Grandad used to grow them in their garden especially for her. He had died some years before I was born so I never knew him, but these little gestures suggest that theirs had been a close and loving relationship, although their lives had been one of poverty & hardship and sometimes of deep pain, with the loss of at least three of their children.

Our route would take us over the Mill Suspension Bridge and into Priory Terrace, where we would pause a moment to drop a few copper coins into the lifeboat-shaped collection box, hanging above a hedge fronting one of the houses. From there we would call in at a tiny sweet shop in Gloucester Street and Mom would always buy 2oz of fish-shaped sweets for us to suck as we walked along.

In Brunswick Street, we would stop to study the fancy headwear displayed in the window of the hat shop. Like many women at that time the two ladies rarely went out without a hat and quite often my mother would become so used to the feel of hers, that she would forget to take it off again when she got home, thus it was not at all unusual to find her standing over the cooker stirring a pot, with her hat still firmly in place.

We would enter the cemetery by the main gate and walk through the old part to reach the Catholic burial grounds. The moment Granny moved the flower pot on the grave, there would be a small explosion of ants, all frantically rushing hither and thither as they sought to find a new safe place for their eggs. With the new flowers in place and the grave tidied, we might sit for a while before starting the walk home, this time passing through the new part of the cemetery and perhaps stopping at a fresh grave to look at the floral tributes and read the messages.

Occasionally we would visit Granny's sister, Sophia. My mother always referred to her as "Yer Aunt Soph" but my less than perfect hearing heard this as "Yer Aunt SOAP", which I thought a very odd name, and it was years before I realised my mistake! Other times we would visit Granny's elder daughter, my Aunt Nance. She had married a soldier and lived at Budbrooke Barracks near Warwick, during the early days of her marriage. My mother told me that once a week, Nance would walk to Leamington to do her shopping and visit the family... then my teenage mom would be given the task of walking back to the Barracks with her, to help push the baby's pram and carry the shopping. After a suitable period of rest, she would then have to walk back to Leamington, but this time she would be escorted by two young soldiers detailed to accompany her and get her home safely. Lucky Mom!

We also visited Aunt Nell quite a lot. Married to granny's son, Alf, she was a tiny, hollow-eyed lady who always seemed rather sad. When I was old enough to understand, Mom explained that Alf had gone missing, presumed dead, whilst serving with the army during the war. For a good while nothing was heard of him, until the day he surfaced helping to bury the bodies in one of the concentration camps. I remember him as a tall man with jet-black wavy hair and startlingly blue eyes that always seemed to shine with laughter whenever we encountered him driving his dustcart around Leamington town centre.

There was great excitement in the air; Rene was getting married and Pat and I felt quite sure that we were going to be bridesmaids – but we were wrong. There was to be only one maid for the bride and she was the teenage niece of Rene's husband-to-be. If we were disappointed to learn this, then we must have been even more so when we were told that with the wedding scheduled for Boxing Day,

Christmas was being cancelled that year. There simply wasn't the money for both.

Like many working-class weddings at that time the reception was held at home, and so it was that early on Boxing Day morning, most of the furniture was removed from our front room and replaced with trestle tables and benches borrowed from the Salvation Army Citadel next door. White sheets became tablecloths for the day, and the tables were set with borrowed cutlery and china. Uncle Tom and Auntie Beat provided the wedding cake and this was delivered by Uncle Tom in the coffin-shaped sidecar of his motorbike, which was normally used for delivering bread orders.

I'd been looking forward with excitement to the wedding but with space in the front room being at a premium, I found myself confined to the kitchen and young brother-sitting duties, but then my mother unexpectedly thrust some money into my hand and instructed me to take Tom to the pictures "out of the way".

Hip, Hip, Hooray! By now I'd worked out that weddings were actually quite boring and I was more than happy to leave the grown-ups to it and spend the afternoon in the company of Doris Day and Calamity Jane.

There were three cinemas in Leamington at that time. The one I was most familiar with was the Clifton Cinema in Spencer Street which held Saturday morning picture shows for children. Sometimes it would be a comedy film featuring Laurel & Hardy or Old Mother Riley, perhaps.

Then again it might be cowboys and Indians with Roy Rodgers or Gene Autry taking centre stage, whilst Gabby Hayes provided a humorous element.

The Regent was probably the biggest cinema. Situated in the middle of Regent Grove, there always seemed to be long queues of people waiting to get in, which often reached right down to the Town Hall. It was the custom at the time for the National Anthem to be played at the end of the evening's viewing, during which the cinema-goers were expected to show their respects for the Royal family by standing to attention until the last notes had faded away. Those who did not wish to do so or were perhaps simply afraid of missing the last bus home, would leave the cinema shortly before the film ended, thus, not only missing the end of the film themselves, but also disrupting the viewing of everyone else.

If one did miss the bus then there were taxis available from the rank on the Holly Walk, but with pubs closing around 10.30 pm, and their clientele adding to the queues, there could be a lengthy wait.

My favourite picture House was the Regal. Situated on a corner site at the end of Augusta Place, it reached from Portland Place In the north to Dormer Place in the south, and was a very elegant building built in art deco style. And, since few people had cars at that time, the architects had very thoughtfully included bicycle racks, built into the Augusta Place side.

We got our money's worth when visiting the cinema in those days since, in addition to the main film, there would be a shorter B class movie included in the programme, together with the latest Pathe News.

During the intermissions, uniformed usherettes would take up positions at the front of the auditorium and sell small tubs of ice-cream from trays suspended round their necks.

There had been a fourth cinema In Upper Bedford Street but this closed in 1952. After demolition, a spacious open plan store was built on the site, and A H Hayes (Furnishers) moved in. (The building is still there, but now it is a branch of Lee-Longlands.) Officially the cinema was named The Scala but was usually referred to by locals as The Fleapit. Browsing the internet, it would seem that just about every town had a fleapit and ours was far from being the only one.

There were two Leamington newspapers during my growing years – three, if you count The Leamington edition of The Coventry Evening Telegraph. Printed daily, this was really a Coventry newspaper and was mainly filled with Coventry news, but the first few pages of the Leamington edition were always devoted to the town and the surrounding areas. Their offices were to be found in a rather lovely building on the south-east corner of The Parade and Regent Street, the onetime home of the L & N W Railway parcel office.

I believe they employed the young roving photographer who could often be spotted around town looking for photo opportunities. One afternoon I was with two school friends studying the paintings in the Art Gallery, when he happened along and asked us to pose for him. He being such a familiar face to us, we readily did so, but I don't think the photo ever got used. I suspect not.

Usually just four pages long, The Morning News was also a daily paper. The front page was devoted to local news stories and the back, to advertisements. These could be announcements of Births, Deaths and Marriages, or of Coming-of-Age. Most importantly perhaps, it contained the job adverts. Inside, there might be sports results, or details of local funerals, which could include the names of the mourners.

The photo-filled windows of their offices could be found in Upper Bedford Street, sandwiched between the back entrances of Woolworths and Marks and Spencer.

The Leamington Spa Courier was a weekly paper satisfyingly filled with local news and in-depth sports reports covering several pages long. In addition to the personal and job advertisements, it usually featured pages covering local weddings. These were very detailed, featuring not only a photo of the bride and groom, but information about when and where the wedding took place, who the parents were and the names of the bridesmaids and best-man. They might even mention where the bride and groom were going for their honeymoon.

For those looking to buy a house, this paper was indispensable as it featured a thick, centre pull-out, filled with advertisements from all the estate agents in town.

The Courier offices were in Lower Bedford Street, on the corner of Portland Road, but should you chance to walk down that narrow side street, you would have found the Courier Press Works taking up most of its northern side. On hot days the doors were often left open giving a tantalising glimpse of the printing machines in operation.

Chapter Fourteen
The Dentist's Chair

I took to school as easily as a duck takes to water. Right from the very first day I loved going, but there was one morning when I was just too miserable with toothache to concentrate on my lessons and while the other children bent their heads over their slates, I rested mine on my arms and sobbed quietly.

In a time when few homes could boast the telephone, contacting my mother, who might, in any case, be gossiping in any one of the many shops that formed our town centre, would not have been easy. This being so, Sister Catherine simply took matters into her own hands by telephoning the School Dental Clinic and arranging for me to be seen straight away.

The job of delivering me there was given to my sister who, unlike me, had no great liking for school and would normally have been delighted to find herself so unexpectedly set free from the classroom, but, for some reason that I didn't then understand, on that particular morning she seemed less than happy with the task allotted to her, and so she dawdled me along as slowly as it was possible without coming to a complete standstill.

However, for all that she might delay it, there could be no escaping the inevitable and all too soon we were crossing The Parade and fetching up outside the side-door of a large Victorian mansion. She released my hand and pointed. "In there." she said. "that's where you've got to go". I looked at her wide-eyed with surprise; surely, she was coming in with me? But no. As far as she was concerned, she had done what was required of her by delivering me to the door, and now the rest was up to me.

We argued for a while, then she pushed me towards the door telling me, "Go on, go on in", and with that she turned and walked away. I was not yet five years old and no way was I going into that building by myself, so I ran after her and grabbed her hand. She pushed me away and walked off again. I trotted after her. She turned, stamped her foot and threatened me, then walked away once more; and so, we slowly progressed up the Holly Walk and into Newbold Street, Pat marching determinably along in front, and me, trailing miserably behind.

At the far end of the street a high grey wall formed the garden boundary of another grand Victorian mansion. Inside, a line of heavily pollarded trees stood sentinel, forming darkly sinister shapes against the skyline. As we passed by, Pat lowered her voice to a whisper and warned me that there were ghosts living in that garden and if I didn't do as she said and go back to the dentist's then they would come over the wall and get me!

But even with that threat hanging over my young head, I could not be persuaded to return to the clinic alone. Slowly, we continued making our way around the block until, finally, we found ourselves right back where we had started, standing outside the dentist's door. Once again, we argued, Pat insisting that I go in alone and me stubbornly refusing to do so...It was stalemate.

I did get to see the dentist eventually, but this time it was my mother who took me and so there was to be no escaping my fate. The heavy wooden door was opened in answer to our ring and we were shown into a large and gloomy room where several people sat in unsmiling silence. My normally garrulous Mother sat down on one of the hard, straight-backed chairs lining the walls and nervously joined the unsmiling ones.

Very shortly, a nurse came to fetch me, taking me by the hand and leading me down a corridor and into a room wherein sat an ancient ancestor of the Mastermind chair, placed squarely in the centre of the floor and facing onto a large window. The nurse helped me into the chair and tied a big white bib around my neck, then a white-coated man bent his head over mine, ordered me to open my mouth, and began to poke around inside it with some strange looking instruments.

The examination over, it was decided that the offending tooth must come out there and then and, before I had a chance to protest, a heavy, black rubber mask was clamped over my nose and mouth held firmly in place by a pair of strong hands. The mask smelt unpleasantly odd and I didn't like it one bit. I couldn't breathe and the panic swept over me as I struggled furiously, trying to push the mask away...

Somewhere in the distance I heard a piercing scream... and then I was thrashing about wildly, arms flaying, hitting out at some unseen terror, as bright red blood spluttered from my mouth and ... Quite suddenly, I was fully conscious again and staring down in dismay at the skirt of my pretty rust-coloured dress, now liberally splattered with spots of quickly darkening blood.

Still bleeding and feeling decidedly groggy from the gas, I was ushered into a side room and seated at a small table, but if I was expecting tea and sympathy then I must have been sorely disappointed for, instead of a teapot, the nurse produced an enormous model of the brightest, whitest, set of teeth that I had ever seen, and instantly set about showing me how I should brush my own dainty little set of pearly-whites!

In fact, I didn't own a toothbrush at that time or, indeed, the toothpaste to go on it. These wouldn't feature in our daily lives until several years later when Pat and I were each given toothbrushes and tins of dentifrice one Christmas, courtesy of Sister de Patsy, the nun attached to St Peter's Church.

Schooling in the 40's and 50's was more formal and structured than it is today, but this seemed to suit my personality and, in spite of my shyness, I settled in very quickly. At nine o'clock in the morning a large hand-bell would be rung in the playground, signalling the beginning of the school day. At the sound of it, everyone rushed to line up in single file outside the appropriate doors, and the noisy playground would suddenly become so quiet that a person might almost hear the proverbial pin drop. Once inside the classroom we would stand beside our desks in silence awaiting permission to sit down.

"Good morning children".

"Good morning, Miss".

"You may sit down".

From now on we would work in silence, speaking only when given permission to do so, or putting up a hand and waiting for the teacher to notice, should we need to ask a question. We sat at double desks arranged in neat rows and all facing the teacher, who sat at the front of the class in solitary splendour, at a tall desk raised high on a dais...'All the better to see you with.' perhaps!

St Peter's is a red-brick Victorian building with windows set high up in the walls, so there was little chance for gazing out and day dreaming. The windows were opened and closed by pulling on a loop of stout cord rather as a venetian blind is operated today, and we all thought it a great honour to be chosen for this task.

When I first started at the school it took girls aged from four to fifteen, and small boys until the age of seven, when they would transfer to the boys' school in New Street, but sometime in the late 40's or early 50's, a new school for senior girls was built in Cashmore Avenue, with Sister Agnes appointed as Head Teacher, and St Peter's became an Infants and Juniors school only. I imagine the new school was built in order to more readily accommodate the extra pupils when the school leaving age was raised from fourteen to fifteen in 1948. No doubt my eldest sister, Rene, had been looking forward to leaving as her fourteenth birthday approached, so she must have been very disappointed to find that she now had to stay for an extra year!

It was in that same summer that an older girl approached me in the playground one lunch time, and asked if my sister had left the school now. As Pat could clearly be seen on the other side of the playground, I was puzzled by this.

"Oh, no." said the girl "I don't mean Pat, I mean your other sister."

Now I was totally confused.

"But I haven't got another sister." I protested.

She looked at me strangely.

"Yes, you have." she insisted.

Later, I told Pat about the conversation, and only then did I learn that Rene, the big girl who sometimes came visiting at our house, was, in fact, my eldest sister!

Usually, the whole class would be taught together except for subjects such as spelling and arithmetic, when we would be divided into groups according to ability. We learned our multiplication tables by chanting them out loud, likewise the (Imperial) values of weights and measures, both solids and liquids. We were frequently tested on these and also on spellings, of which we were given a new list to learn each week; there were regular mental arithmetic tests to be faced also.

From the very first, we spent most of the school day working at our studies. To begin with, we simply copied out letters and numbers using slates and chalk, but as we moved further up the school and grew more proficient, we progressed to pencils and paper and then, to pens and exercise books. These were simple dip pens consisting of a nib attached to a wooden handle, much like that of a painting brush. The pens were loaded with ink by dipping them into a small pot of the liquid, but it was always difficult to judge the right amount, too little and the ink would be used up after only one or two words had been written, but too much ink would cause blots to form and make an untidy mess of your work guaranteeing you a ticking off from the teacher.

As a break from the mental work, we might do some drawing; piece together a jigsaw; or model with plasticine, when each child would be given an A4 sized board to work on, together with a golf-ball sized piece of the coloured modelling clay. When the weather was fine, we would go out into the playground for PT lessons or to play games such as 'In and Out the Dusty Bluebells' or 'Oranges & lemons'. For PT, the younger children would play with beanbags, hoops and skipping ropes, but the older girls would be put through an exercise routine that involved lots of bending, stretching and twisting, but it was fun and we all enjoyed those sessions.

All of the teachers at the school were female; all but one, unmarried, and of those, three were nuns. They were Sister Catherine, the Headmistress; Sister Agnes, who taught the older girls and later became headmistress of Cashmore Avenue School, and Sister Marie; who taught those aged 7-8. She was lovely; gentle-faced, serene and kind. As far as I can recall the other teachers rewarded effort by drawing a star on our work, but Sister Marie had a rubber stamp that left an inky imprint of a leopard, and we were all very keen to find those in the pages of our books.

Looking back, I would say that all of our teachers were very nice, and even stern-faced Sister Catherine was more bark than bite, but they were very much of their time; very formal, very strict, and should any child chance to step out of place, then a sharp slap would soon bring him or her back into line.

As we headed towards lunchtime one day, several children raised a hand one after the other to ask to go to the toilet. At first Miss Walsh gave permission but, tiring of so many interruptions to her lesson, she finally declared that the next child to ask for the toilet would get a slap. Unfortunately for me, I already had my hand up and though I put it down again very quickly when faced with this threat, she had already noticed and rounded on me, snapping,

"Yes, Valerie?"

I curled back in my chair, not wanting to answer but feeling compelled to do so by her questioning gaze.

"Please Miss; I want to go to the toilet." I whispered.

She looked at me in astonishment.

"What did I just say?" she demanded, then lifted my arm and delivered a stinging slap to the back of my hand.

"Now go!" she ordered pointing to the door, but I simply burst into tears and, stung by what I considered to be her unfairness, stubbornly refused to budge. As you might guess, after a few minutes the inevitable happened and I spent the rest of the morning sitting in a warm, wet puddle and feeling very uncomfortable indeed.

Every term we had a visit from Nitty Nora, the school nurse, whose job it was to conduct a thorough search of every child's head. There was nothing gentle about this and we dreaded having those probing fingers tugging at our hair. Any child found to be harbouring the little mites would be given a note to take home to their mother. There was no shame in this and we simply regarded nits as a normal part of our childhood. My mother dealt with them by washing our hair with a foul-smelling soap and then dragging a fine-toothed comb through every strand until she was absolutely certain there were none of the tiny creatures left.

We also had regular visits from the school doctor, a rather large lady with very fat fingers that reminded me of sausages. I hated having those fingers touching me and would squirm inwardly, longing for her to be done so that I could escape back to the comforting surrounds of the classroom. When we were due to have vaccinations, my mother would always refuse to sign the consent forms. She didn't like the idea of needles herself and certainly wasn't going to let anybody stick the dreaded things into her children.

One thing I never refused was the daily bottle of school milk. Measuring one third of a pint, it had been introduced in 1946 by the Government of the day, in an attempt to help eradicate the malnutrition so many children were suffering from, following the deprivations of the war years. As there were no fridges in the schools, we drank it as it came, and I have read that in some schools the milk would be sour in the summer months and frozen in the winter, but I don't recall this happening at St Peter's. However, during the winter months, we were given the option of warming our bottles on the central heating pipes that ran round the rooms.

The milk was stopped for senior schools in 1968, by the Wilson Government and then, in 1971, for the over sevens, by the Ted Heath government. As Minister for Education at that time, Margaret Thatcher had the unenviable job of announcing this, earning herself the nickname 'Thatcher, the Milk Snatcher`. In fact, Government papers apparently show that it had been Heath's idea to stop the milk and Mrs Thatcher had actually been against his proposal.

We were nine years old when we made our first garments; a very simple top made from a soft white cotton fabric sprinkled with tiny coloured spots. Two simple T-shapes were cut from the material, with a slight scoop and a vertical slash made at the neck edge of one. Using French seams, we stitched the two pieces together at the sides and shoulders; hemmed the bottom, and bound the armholes and neck with bias binding to match the colour of the spots, leaving a sufficient length of the binding to form a tie. The whole garment was worked by hand and if it wasn't done to Miss Pennington's satisfaction, then out it came, to be worked all over again.

The following year, now in Miss Broadley's class, we were taught embroidery, working rows of different stitches across a piece of fabric. Cross stitch, chain stitch, blanket stitch, feather stitch... each row was worked in a different coloured thread, creating an attractive sample of our work. When finished it was backed by a piece of plain fabric and eventually became a roll to keep knitting needles tidy.

Miss Broadley was said to be the strictest teacher in the school, a reputation no doubt fuelled by the exaggerations of those currently in her class. She was strict, yes, but then to her fell the task of tutoring us for the Eleven Plus Examinations and she worked us hard in preparation for these, but she also introduced us to Dickens, to Scott of the Antarctic, and to Henry the Eighth and his six wives.

On June 30th 1954, the whole school population was gathered together around the bike shed in the lower playground, where it was explained to us that we were about to witness a rare phenomenon – an eclipse of the sun. To help us view it, we were given pieces of coloured cellophane to look through. We now know that this was not a great idea, but no worse, perhaps, than the pieces of dark film negatives or smoked glass that other people recall using.

If we were lacking in good manners when we started at the school, then the teachers made sure that we were well tutored in the little niceties of life whilst in their care. Please and thank you, became automatic responses, but we were also taught to stand up whenever an adult entered the room; to give up our seat if a grown-up was standing, and to hold open doors and let the seniors pass through first; whilst small boys were taught to raise their caps in acknowledgement when passing a lady. Sister Marie also taught us to look after our fingernails; no biting, always keep them neatly trimmed, clean them, and gently push back the cuticles.

We rarely left the building once the school day had begun, but there was one occasion in 1953, when we were all assembled in the playground and then marched down to the Regal Cinema to watch a film showing the Coronation of Queen Elizabeth II. At that time, television screens were tiny, so to see The Coronation on a cinema-sized screen was a great privilege indeed.

During my final year, I was asked to look after a young boy after school, until his mother arrived home from her job in the haberdashery department at Woodward's, a large department store on the corner of The Parade and Regent Street. The father was a projectionist at the Clifton Cinema in Spencer Street, but the family lived in a flat above the Regal Cinema in Augusta Place.

They were very much a middle-class family with middle-class ways and manners. One of Mrs F's sisters was married to Basil, a surgeon at one of the London hospitals, whilst the other was a rather glamorous lady who drove an open top sports car and lived in Redcar, which I always thought sounded terribly posh.

Mr F had a fascinating way of raising just one eyebrow, which he did frequently when reading his copy of The Times. Whenever he came across something that surprised or intrigued him, up the eyebrow would go, so high that it might well have disappeared into his hair – if the front of his head had boasted any for it to disappear into!

Below the flat was a small shop which bore the title 'Radio Rentals'. In spite of its name, it actually rented out television sets and we were allowed to go into the shop after school each evening to watch the children's programmes, thus I was introduced to The Woodentops and The Flowerpot men.

Another 'perk of the job' was that not only did we get into the Saturday morning pictures for free; we also got to sit in 'The Box'. This was a raised, enclosed area at the back of the circle and at other times it might well be occupied by courting couples, for being the most expensive place to sit, it was where a young man who had fallen badly, might take the girl he was out to impress.

Chapter Fifteen
St Peter's Church

Standing in the middle of St Peter's Hall, I watched enviously as mothers and nuns arranged delicate white veils and pretty head-dresses on the young girls who would shortly be taking part in the procession around the Pump Room Gardens. Sister Marie saw me looking and smiled, "Let us see if we can't find something for you." she said, delving into a box and producing a pretty blue and white circlet of flowers. She placed it on my head then stood back and admired her choice, before handing me over to an older girl and instructing her to let me walk with her in the procession. Really, I was far too young to take part and I was thrilled that I was being allowed to do so.

St Peter's being a Roman Catholic School, religion played a large part in our daily lives. We started and ended our days with prayers, were well drilled in the Catechism and endlessly practised the hymns we would sing at Benediction on Thursday afternoons, when the whole school population would be marched down to the church for the last hour of the school day.

From time to time, missionaries would visit the school to tell of their work in Africa and India and encourage us to donate money to help fund this. We were also expected to raise money for the Father Hudson's Children's Homes in Birmingham, and once a year we would be given an A4 sheet of card with twelve small envelopes attached to the front. We were told that we had to put at least one penny in each envelope before handing it back; however, it was always stressed that we mustn't just ask our parents for the money, but must show a degree of effort by earning it ourselves.

On Sunday mornings we were expected to go to the 9 o'clock Mass which was said in English and geared especially towards children. Should you fail to attend then you could be sure that the priest's beady eyes would notice your absence and come Monday morning he would be at the school and, in front of the whole class, demand to know why he hadn't seen YOU at Mass yesterday.

Between the ages of seven and eight we were prepared for our First Holy Communion. Again and again, we practised walking down the centre aisle, kneeling at the altar rails and, hands clasped in prayer, opening our mouths wide and putting out our tongues ready to receive the Host. Then we would rise quietly to our feet and, with hands still clasped and eyes lowered, we would make our way back to the pews via the side aisles. But before we could make our First Communion, we must make our First Confession, and again we would practise and practise, until Sister was sure that we all knew what we had to do.

Being three years older, Pat was the first of we two to make our Communion, but I recall going with my mother to buy her a dress from Bradshaw's in Regent Street, which was almost certainly paid for with the aid of a Provident cheque*. Later, when my turn came, I would also wear the dress for both my First Communion and for Confirmation.

This shop was also the local suppler for Guide, Brownie, Scout & Cub uniforms, with one window always being filled with every article of uniform and piece of equipment that any Guide or Scout might ever need, be it a penknife or a new badge to sew on a sleeve.

The headquarters of the Leamington, Kenilworth and Southam Boy Scouts Association could be found next door at No 105**. Inside, there appeared to be some kind of meeting hall and, attached to the window, there always seemed to be a notice advising the day and time of the next Beetle Drive. This intrigued me. What was that? And how do you drive a beetle?

At that time, we were required to fast before taking Communion and so there would be no pre-Mass breakfast for the new young communicants that morning; however, following the Mass, the school provided a veritable feast of a breakfast, the like of which some of us would never have seen before.

Breakfast over, we went home to change and then reassembled at the church a while later, where we boarded a coach and set off for an afternoon of pleasure. Pat went to Wicksteed Park in Northamptonshire and she came home filled with excitement and stories of her day. I was quite jealous and longed to go to this wonderful place she was describing, so when my turn came, I found myself tingling with anticipatory pleasure as I boarded the coach, convinced that I, too, was about to enjoy an afternoon at the Park.

Off we went along Dormer Place, turned into the Parade and then into Old Warwick Road, excitement building all the time, but this was to be short-lived for in no time at all, the coach was pulling up and I was totally dismayed to find that we were to go no further than Warwick Park! Now, there was nothing wrong with Warwick Park. Indeed, I loved going there, but it was something of a let-down when I had been expecting something more.

Of course, once there, we enjoyed ourselves enormously, playing on the swings and paddling in the stream that runs through the park to the river - and having the luxury of a coach to transport us there and back, did compensate to a certain degree. Usually, we walked to the park or we might catch a bus if we could scrabble together enough pennies to pay the fare. More memorable were those two or three occasions when we children discovered that we had enough pennies gathered between us, to allow the excitement of travelling from Leamington to Warwick by train!

The next big religious occasion in our lives was Confirmation. Pat was sponsored by Claire Willes, a member of the local Squire's family, and I, by her sister, Eleanor. The sisters lived together in Newbold Terrace, in a large, double-fronted detached house, which overlooked the Jephson Gardens. How they came to sponsor us, I know not for we did not mix with them socially, nor did they ever take any interest in us, either before our confirmations or after, except for one time, when I was sent to their house to collect a box of apples from their garden. The housekeeper let me in, and bade me sit on a chair in the hall, before disappearing through one of the doorways. A short time later, she returned carrying a cardboard box filled with windfalls. Of the sisters, there was no sign.

Tom was still a baby when our mother was offered a job as cleaner at St Peter's Church. If Granny was unable to look after him, then Mom would simply take him with her and he would spend the morning in the sacristy, where he was fussed over by Sister de Patsy and the ladies who came in to polish the brasses or arrange the flowers.

During the school holidays, I would often go along too, happy to help with any little jobs they could find for me. A favourite task was to scrape off the candle wax from the offertory stands that stood at various points around the church, and then to fill up the attached cans with fresh candles. Another job that I loved was to polish the wooden base beneath the crucifix hanging opposite to the main entrance. I considered this to be my special job and I took great pleasure in making it shine. One job I didn't enjoy so much was being sent up into the organ gallery to dust. I found it very spooky being alone up there and would always run across the darkened area between the top of the stairs and the gallery itself, convinced that if I hesitated for a moment, then I would surely be accosted by the ghost of some long dead organist!

At that time, the church kneelers were long wooden affairs that stretched from one end of a pew to the other and often, my mother would enlist my help to lift them up onto the benches so that she could clean the floor beneath.

Sometimes we would find a forgotten prayer book or rosary beads and, quite frequently, a dropped coin or two. The prayer books and rosary beads would be placed on a table near to the door ready to be reclaimed by the owners, but the dropped coins would very quickly find their way into the pocket of Mom's apron, as she considered them to be a much welcome perk of the job. It may not have been the right thing to do, but there were times when those coins must have helped put food into our bellies.

There were four priests at the church during my childhood years; Father Flint, Father Stanz, Father Corrigan and Father Kelly. We saw very little of the two senior men except at Mass, but the two younger men seemed to be much more involved with parochial affairs. A darkly handsome young man, Father Corrigan was a Scout leader and could often be seen out and about in his uniform of khaki shirt and knee-length shorts, which revealed a pair of sturdy, masculine legs heavily covered by thick dark hair.

Father Kelly was very different. A tall, slim young man, he was inclined to let his hair down when not 'on duty', and often acted more like a big brother than a priest, tickling and teasing me, or hoisting me up onto his shoulders and charging around the sacristy, laughing and whooping with glee. Although it was fun, at the same time I found it quite embarrassing, simply because it just didn't seem right for a priest to be behaving that way.

My parents' marriage was a 'mixed marriage' insofar as Mom was a Catholic, whilst Dad always claimed to be Chapel. In fact, he was baptised at St Mary's Church in Cubbington, but might well have converted at some stage. Whatever his religious upbringing, he seemed not to adhere very closely to any particular religious group and, during my younger days, Sunday evenings would always find him outside the Town hall joining in the Salvation Army service, often with me sitting on his shoulders. One of Dad's brothers was a Salvationist and I rather feel that had he been able to give up the drink, then Dad would have joined him there. At any rate, although Pat and I were Catholic, he insisted that we go to Sunday School at the Citadel.

I remember one occasion when the whole congregation gathered together and marched to the Baptist Church in Warwick Street to take part in some kind of inter-denominational service, but I never did take part in this because we hadn't been there long when my nose started to bleed. Help was soon to hand when two ladies took charge and led me down to the dark and gloomy basement where they swiftly administered their own brand of emergency first aid, by dropping a large bunch of keys down the back of my dress.

As far as my mother was concerned, it would be more accurate to say that she was a lapsed Catholic since she only ever went to Mass on those occasions that absolutely demanded it. She always said that she spent enough time in church during the week and didn't see what difference it made if she didn't go on Sundays.

(**NO 135 REGENT STREET later became Toytown, said to be the biggest independent toy shop in the country, and remembered today with great fondness, both by my own children and by others of similar age.

*PROVIDENT CHEQUES were small loans which came in the form of vouchers to be exchanged for goods at participating shops. An agent working for the Provident Company, would arrange the loans and then call at the house each week to collect repayments.)

Chapter Sixteen
Leamington Girl's College

The letter arrived one morning in the early summer of 1954. My Mother picked up the official-looking brown envelope and frowned as she turned it over and over in her hands before finally opening it and extracting the contents. She read the letter slowly; her face lighting up with surprise as she did so, then she looked at me." Yer've passed fer the Girls' College." she said.

That she was proud of me there was no doubt, for in the days that followed she boasted unashamedly of my achievement to friends and strangers alike, but maternal pride must have sat side by side with major worry, for there was simply no way that my impoverished parents could afford to buy the exclusive and extensive uniform.

Outdoor shoes and indoor shoes, navy velour hat with striped band for winter; straw hat with ditto for summer; the list seemed endless, but Mom did her best and by September I was the proud owner of one second-hand, vee-neck tunic in the regulation french navy; two second-hand vee-neck blouses, the sleeves of which had been cropped short at the elbows by the previous owner; one second-hand hat, a little faded and somewhat battered, and one second-hand blazer, the latter two items both kindly donated, but the blazer massively overlarge for my tiny eleven year old frame, having previously been owned by a sixteen year old who had left school behind her at the end of the previous term.

Feeling both excited and nervous, I made my way to school on the first day of term balancing unsteadily on a pair of Cuban-heeled shoes belonging to my mother, who had failed in her attempts to find me a new pair of second-hand school shoes. A red pump bag, fashioned from an old jumper, bumped against my legs, and from my left shoulder hung my most treasured possession, the brand-new canvas satchel Mom and I had bought from Rawlinson's.

Being the youngest of three girls, brand new rarely travelled in my direction, so to find myself the owner of something which still bore the heady scent of newness, was an exciting experience. Again and again, I tenderly ran my fingers across the canvass, glorifying in its newness. Sometimes I would practise walking back and forth across the bedroom floor nonchalantly swinging the bag from my shoulder. Should I wear it a little lower perhaps – or a little higher; on my right shoulder; or on my left? Pride simply knew no bounds.

Taking my place in the classroom for the first time, I looked around with interest at my new classmates and noted with some surprise that everyone was dressed identically in the regulation uniform. Everyone that is, except me. It was to be my first intimation that I was somehow different.

Barely had I time to notice this before the door opened, and in walked two prefects armed with notebooks and pencils. We were instructed to empty the contents of our satchels and pump bags onto our desks and then the prefects began to move around the room visiting each girl in turn, not only to check that she had every piece of uniform and equipment required, but that all were properly labelled with her name. Needless to say, I was lacking in both areas and so it was that the following morning I found myself joining the group of girls already silently assembled outside Miss Waterfield's study.

As I entered the room she gazed at me over the top of her half-moon spectacles, eyes filling with distaste as she took in my somewhat shambolic appearance, then she turned back to her desk and studied the note book lying there. The ticking of a clock punctuated the silence and several long minutes passed by before she turned back to me again and demanded to know why I was missing so much of the uniform. Quivering beneath the coldness of her gaze, I stammered a reply, explaining that my mother couldn't afford everything; but this, it seemed, was not an acceptable reason and simply brushing it aside, she instructed me to remind my mother that the uniform was compulsory and I must have everything.

Mom listened in silence as I told her of my visit to Miss Waterfield's room and repeated the message. Then she exploded, jabbing her finger vigorously into the space between us as she shouted, "Oh! Your 'eadmistress said that, did she? Well, you can just go and tell your 'eadmistress from me that if she wants you to 'ave these things, she can bloody well go and buy 'em for you 'erself."

And that was that as far as Mom was concerned. But not so for me, as the invitations to visit to Miss Waterfield's inner sanctum were repeated at the start of every single term throughout my time at the school. Whether or not she ever took the matter up with my parents directly, I do not know. Certainly, my mother never mentioned it, so one can only assume not.

What, then, did the headmistress gain from those pointless visits? At 11 years old, I did not have the money to buy the uniform for myself, nor were my hard-working but poorly-paid parents, able to conjure up the money from nowhere. One can only imagine therefore, that she felt a certain pleasure and sense of her own importance, from bullying her young charges in that manner. A more compassionate woman might surely have asked parents to donate outgrown uniforms to the school, to be offered to those girls from poorer backgrounds?

On the same day that I first became acquainted with the interior of Miss Waterfield's room, I also met Miss Absolum, the geography mistress. A rather sour-faced woman, she habitually wore gown and mortar board as, indeed, did most of the senior teachers including the two male members of staff, Mr Gee, who taught Latin to the girls from year 3 upwards, and a younger man who taught music.

At the end of that first geography lesson, we were told to draw a map for homework, marking the rivers and roads in colour. Unfortunately, this presented a problem for me as I did not have any colouring pencils, nor did I know anyone who did. I was far too shy to ask any of my new classmates for a loan of theirs, so I did the only thing I could think to do, and drew the whole map using an ordinary graphite affair. Miss Absolum was not impressed and demanded to know why I hadn't coloured the map.

"I haven't got any crayons, Miss"

"Then borrow some!" she barked "and stay behind for an hour's train prep." This was designed for girls who used public transport, providing a safe place for them to wait and to get started on their homework, but it was also used for the detention of miscreants such as myself. I was doing well. Only two days into my new school and already I had a visit to the head's study and a detention under my belt!

Miss Absolom and I just did not get on. She clearly disliked the skinny little ragbag of a child who had landed in her midst and when a cold brought on a severe coughing fit in class one day, she immediately banished me to the furthest reaches of the classroom and ordered me to stand with my face turned into the corner for the rest of the lesson. As time went on, I became so nervous of her that I started to become physically sick even by the thought of going into her lessons, and I spent several mornings in sick bay. Eventually, it all became too much. I just could not face going to school on geography days and I began to play truant.

My Mother was in the habit of leaving the small kitchen window open when she went out believing that no-one could possibly squeeze through such a small space. What she didn't seem to realise was that by standing on the outflow pipe from the sink, it was possible to reach an arm through and undo the catch of the larger side window, thus allowing easy access to the house. Knowing this, I would hide until Mom went out and then I would slip inside and stay there until I judged it was time to be making myself scarce again. After that, I would hang around out of sight until I saw other children coming home from school and then I would go home as though I, too, had been at school all day.

In truth, it wasn't just the antipathy of the two ladies that was causing me to be unhappy at school. If I'm to be honest, then I have to admit that I was just completely out of my depth and simply didn't fit in. Coming from my background, I had not the knowledge, the vocabulary, the verbal or the social skills, to gain full advantage of my time there. Unfortunately, my parents seemed not to realise the struggle I was having and were totally unsupportive. Indeed, their attitude towards me just added to my problems.

My father, for instance, always considered school to be a complete waste of time, often declaring, "I went in, in standard two an' I cem out in standard two, an' it never did me no 'arm." totally ignoring the fact that his lack of education had forced him into a life of hard physical work for which he received very little recompense. From the start he was infuriated that I had homework to do. "I thought I told you not t' bring bloody school work 'ome 'ere my wench.", he would shout whenever he caught me out, and I very quickly learned to keep my books out of sight when he was around.

At school we had elocution lessons on a weekly basis and so I learned to round my vowels and pronounce my aitches. One exercise was for each girl to write a short essay and then to read it aloud to the rest of the class, who would then be invited to pick fault with her diction. My accent must have been quite challenging, evolving as it did from a mix of local village accents that had trickled down through my father's line from places such as Hampton Lucy, Stoneleigh, Kenilworth, Wolston and Grandborough; before finally ending up in Cubbington, where Dad was born and raised.

My mother's lineage was more complicated harking back to the Eastend of London, Watford, Bushey and Waddesdon down one branch; Whitnash, Wasperton, Anstruther and Ireland (Rosscommon?) down others. She herself was born in Leamington, but her father was a Cockney and she had spent several of her childhood years living in Camberwell, where she attended Cork Street School. However, she was wont to show her Scots ancestry by cutting us satisfyingly thick "pieces", or even "jelly pieces", whenever her housekeeping money stretched to a jar of jam. And when she was cross with me, "my lass" was often her chosen term of address, whilst Dad would settle for a stern Warwickshire, "my wench."

"Yer yampy buggers" was an expression he used when Pat and I were fooling about, and if he was going to bed, he would declare that he was "goin' up t' wooden 'ill." But possibly one of his most memorable expressions was the warning he always gave that he was "goin' t' the shit'us," thus ensuring that we would all be aware that the lavatory would be occupied for the next while.

My parents were not impressed by my new speech patterns and took to calling me "the snob". It didn't help matters that one day, deeply engrossed in conversation with my friends; I inadvertently passed Mum by in the street. When I protested that I simply hadn't seen her, she would have none of it. "Yer gettin' too big fer yer boots, my lass." she declared, and would scathingly tell her acquaintances of my short comings, commenting, "She thinks she's too good for us now she's a college girl."

Looking back from this distance I can see that, unfamiliar with the ways of the higher education system, they, too, were out of their depth and it must have been a stressful time for them also. They were proud of their young daughter and it must have hit them badly that they couldn't provide adequately for her as she entered her new school life. We were well aware of our poverty, after all we lived it every day, but now we were having our noses well and truly rubbed in it, and I was made to feel ashamed. Then too, being poorly educated themselves, they would have been unable to help with my school work, lacking the knowledge or the understanding, and at times they must surely have felt that they were losing their daughter.

Of course, my time at the school wasn't all bad, and the teachers were mostly quite pleasant. My favourite was Mrs Cooke, our sports mistress. She also had charge of the sick bay and gave me some much-needed TLC during the mornings I spent there. I quite enjoyed sport but unfortunately my ability didn't match my enthusiasm and if ever a medal had been given for the least able, then surely it would have been mine. The College had a rather lovely gymnasium that ran across the whole width of the basement, but for tennis and hockey, we used the facilities in Victoria Park.

Every football fan will be familiar with the deep roars that punctuate the air around any major stadium during a match, but the volume of noise produced is surely as nothing when compared to that emanating from the thousands of teenage girls who had gathered at the old Wembley Stadium to watch the Hockey International between England and Wales, on 12th March 1955. Although new to hockey and still unfamiliar with the rules, I was amongst those girls but, in truth, although I enjoyed the day, I found the match itself rather disappointing simply because we were just too far distant to get a good view in such a big stadium.

If unfamiliar with the rules then, I have forgotten them completely now and today I have only two memories of playing the game; one, is that I always seemed to end the lessons all bloodied and bleeding from the blisters that my second-hand hockey stick wore on my hands, and the other is that a whack on the ankle from a hockey stick, jolly well HURTS!

Perhaps because one had to pass the 11 plus examination in order to get into Grammar School, many people seemed to assume that the curriculum was all academic, but that wasn't so. For instance, we had needlework lessons, during which we made pale blue cotton tunics to wear in our dance classes. Now, you might think that these classes would have covered the social dances, providing us with a possibly useful skill to take into our adult lives, but you would be wrong. Instead, we found ourselves prancing around the hall waving our arms in the air and, pretending to be trees. They were fun lessons and a welcome break from French verbs, but I doubt if many girls went on to have careers in dancing.

We also made neat little gingham aprons and caps to wear during cookery lessons. I can't recall now what we cooked, but I do remember one girl leaving her still-baking cakes in charge of the teacher, only for the teacher to promptly forget all about them until reminded by the smell of burning!

Art was another favourite lesson but, again, my abilities and my enthusiasm were totally mismatched. There are vague memories of producing a simple watercolour picture and of getting messy with papier mache; I can also recall making a mosaic plaque using eggshells that we had crushed and dyed in a variety of colours. One sunny afternoon saw us sitting by the paddling pool in Victoria Park sketching the young children playing there. Our teacher, no doubt as glad to be out of the classroom as we were, wandered among us stopping to comment and advise. Reaching me, she looked over my shoulder at the matchstick figure I had drawn and then, pointing out that small children had rounded bodies and limbs, she took my pencil from me and made a few deft strokes on the paper to illustrate. How easy she made it look and how I envied her ability.

In the chemistry lab we learned that blue litmus paper turned red in acidic conditions, and red litmus paper turned blue under alkaline conditions, whilst in the neighbouring biology lab, we were taught about the life cycle of the frog. When we moved on to spiders, we were tasked with bringing one into school to study. This was homework I had no problems with, since we shared our outside loo with a good number of them and I was able to find a lovely fat garden spider without any trouble at all.

The corridor outside the laboratories was hung with coat hooks for our lab coats. These were smart royal blue affairs and looked very professional. All, that is, except for mine, which was actually a maternity smock that my mother had worn when she was pregnant with my brother. Although it was indeed royal blue, the colourful array of flowers decorating the fabric made it look anything but professional and it stood out a mile!

I was appointed ink monitor for my form which meant staying behind every afternoon to fill the china inkwells in our desks. The oilcans containing the ink were lined up on the steps outside the caretaker's room, and had to be replaced there when we had finished, ready for hm to refill the following day. School ink was blue/black and made from a mixture of powder and water. It wasn't very nice and some girls would have their own bottles of Quink – a commercial ink available from stationers. Each desk had a hole cut into the top on the right-hand side into which the china well fitted. There was no provision for left handers, but fortunately, as we had left our dip pens behind us at junior school and were all using fountain pens by then, this wasn't so much of a problem.

My ears were a constant source of trouble when I was young and I vaguely remember Mom taking me to the Warneford Hospital to see a consultant one time. Almost certainly this would have been after the birth of the NHS in 1948 and was possibly her first experience of visiting the hospital. Rather lacking in confidence in many ways and used to self-medicating, she would have found this a nerve-racking experience and certainly not one she would have wanted to repeat. That being so, when an abscess formed in my ear and burst, leaving me with a thick, smelly discharge, she would have been reluctant to take me to the doctor and risk another hospital visit, so she simply cleaned up the mess from around my ear each morning and plugged it with cotton wool, no doubt hoping that it would eventually clear itself.

Then one morning, my form mistress noticed and asked if I had seen the doctor about it. When I replied that I hadn't, she said she thought that I should, and to ask my mother to take me. My heart sank. This, I knew, would not please Mom, so when I nervously broached the subject with her that evening, I was fully prepared for her reaction, "Oh, your teacher said that, did she? Well, you can tell your teacher from me, I'll decide when you need t' see a doctor, not 'er!"

Miss Morse seemed surprised to see me in school the following day and asked again if I had seen my doctor. "No Miss", I cringed. Then, not wanting to repeat my mother's words, I added "Mommy said she'd take me when she has time."

Nothing more was said but after lunch that day, I was summoned to Miss Waterfield's study. As usual I found myself trembling with nerves as I waited outside her door but, to my surprise, I wasn't getting a ticking off. Instead, I was told to get my coat as she was taking me home. It seems that she had taken it upon herself to phone the doctor and had arranged for him to visit me at home that afternoon. He duly arrived and gave me a shot of penicillin together with instructions to stay home for the next week, as he would be coming back every day to administer more.

I do not know what was said by Miss Waterfield to my mother as I was sent out into the kitchen while they talked, but Mom would certainly not have been happy to have the Headmistress confront her in her own home. Whatever was said, sometime later - oh, joy of joys - I was told that I would not be returning to the school after the end of that term.

(During the years when I was a pupil at the school, the College was to be found at the rear of the old Leamington Library & Museum in Avenue Road, occupying all three floors of the building, including the basement gymnasium. However; in September 1958, it moved house, taking possession of a brand new, purpose-built building on the northern outskirts of the town. Meanwhile, Clapham

Terrace Senior school was also on the move, taking over the old College buildings temporarily, whilst a new school was built to replace it. More new schools were built in the years that followed, including one on the Whitnash side of town to replace the old Campion School in Leicester Street.)

Chapter Seventeen
Moving House

Tom was ill, and on this occasion our parents were sufficiently concerned to send for the doctor. They had expected Dr Fogarty to come but instead it was her young nephew who had just joined her in the practice. He diagnosed pneumonia and double bronchitis, and for a while it was very much touch and go for our small brother. He did survive, but Dr Powell had not been impressed by our living conditions and wrote to the Council suggesting that we should be rehoused as a matter of urgency. And so it was that I arrived home from school one lunch time, to find Pat standing outside the house reading that day's copy of the Morning News, her face a picture of concern. "They're going to knock our house down" she said, "Look! It says so here, in the Morning News".

We moved on a miserably wet Friday in April, 1955, some 26 years after my parents had first applied to go on the Council's housing list. The house was so new that the builders were still working on the maisonettes that bookended our new home and the footpaths had not yet been made, leaving us with the prospect of picking our way through a sea of thick gloopy mud in order to reach the front door. Luckily some of the builders were still on site and they quickly came to our rescue by laying a carpet of scaffolding planks from the road to the house.

It didn't take long to move our few possessions and soon the removal men were gone and we were able to explore our new home properly. The ground floor offered a long narrow living room stretching from the front to the back of the house, with windows at either end to let in plenty of light. A door at the rear end led into the kitchen/diner and from there we could access the store room and the understairs cupboard. Upstairs, there were three bedrooms; two doubles and a single. There was also a bathroom containing a long white bath and a wash basin, and next door to that was a lavatory.

For the first time we experienced the luxury of electricity and indoor plumbing, and we could even have hot water on tap by means of the back-boiler behind the fire in the living room. This also heated the radiator in the kitchen; but we could only enjoy these luxuries during the winter months when a fire was lit. During the summer months, preparing a bath required a little more effort since we had to heat our bath water in the gas boiler that came as part of the kitchen furniture. First of all, bucket after bucket of water had to be drawn from the cold tap over the sink and emptied into the boiler; then came a lengthy wait whilst the water heated. Finally, we would transfer it upstairs to the bathroom by the bucketful. It all took a great deal of time and effort, so mostly we would just settle for a kettle of hot water and a strip-down wash at the basin.

Although we were delighted with our new home, it was a good way out of town and there was not yet a bus service to the area, with the current one terminating at the

Pound Lane end of Gresham Avenue, whilst our new home was at the far end of Buckley Road. At first Mom tried walking Tom to school at St Peter's, but it was a long way for a small child and somehow, she never seemed to get the timing quite right, so that he was often late and would then (apparently) be banished to the cloakroom as punishment. She was furious when she found out about this but not accepting any blame for his lateness herself, she declared that "Your teachers should understand that we don't 'ave t' come from just round the corner like some of them do."

She claimed to have had words with the teacher, although I doubt that very much. Nevertheless, Tom was removed from St Peter's and transferred to Lillington School instead. This caused another problem as she could not now get to her job on time and so she gave in her notice and left.

Having lived at The Holt during her younger years, Mom was very familiar with the area and she told us that our new home was built on land that had previously formed part of Lillington Stud farm. Owned by Mr Sydney McGregor, one of two brothers who owned much of the land in Lillington at that time, the Stud was highly successful, breeding up to one hundred horses a year which were sold all over the world, and to such high-profile clients as the Queen Mother and the Aga Khan. Some of the Horses went on to win the racing world's most prestigious races such as The Grand National, The Cheltenham Gold Cup, The Grand Prix de Paris and, perhaps most famously, The Derby in 1932, with a horse named April the fifth, which had been born on Sydney's 40th birthday. Sydney died on the 4th April

1970, the day before his eighty first birthday, and the remaining Stud land became home to a development of new houses between Valley Road and Parklands Avenue, all of which are to be found in roads bearing the names of famous racecourses.

When the Council estate was completed, it boasted more facilities than might be found in many of the small villages around and about. There was a well-appointed shopping centre, a Police Station, and a Pub. This was named The Walnut Tree and was run by Jack Draper, a cousin to my father. There was also an NHS Clinic, a Community Centre, an attractive library and a Roman Catholic Church.

Although family-sized houses made up the bulk of the estate, there were also a few bungalows and several blocks of flats which were mainly to be found in the Mason Avenue area. The tallest of these was the impressive, fourteen storey, Eden Court. This was almost certainly named after Sir Anthony Eden, who was the Member of Parliament for Warwick & Leamington from 1923 – 1957, and Prime Minister for two of those years from 1955 – 1957, when he retired for health reasons. He served as Foreign Secretary under Winston Churchill both during World War 2 and again between 1951 and 1955, when Churchill resigned, and Sir Anthony subsequently became Prime Minister. Although he was an immensely popular politician, sadly he is chiefly remembered for his role in the Suez Crisis. The flats can be seen for miles around and have become something of a local landmark.

Surprisingly, just some thirty years or so after they were built, some of the five-storey blocks were demolished and replaced by smaller units, which it was hoped would appeal to those older tenants who were still living in the family-sized homes, long after their offspring had flown the nest.

Towards the end of 1955, my eldest sister and her husband had also moved to Lillington, taking Granny along with them. By this time, she was very ill and sadly it was an illness from which she would never recover. Just after tea one evening in March 1956, the door opened and Ray burst in, "She's gone" he said. Just two short words, but we all knew what he meant.

I had been kneeling on the floor just inside the door, trying to fashion a blackboard and easel for Tom from some old pieces of wood. I didn't move; just stayed there fiddling with the wood as the tears trickled down my face. It was the first time I had experienced the death of someone I loved and the terrible pain of that loss.

My mother tried to persuade me to go to the undertakers with everyone else to say a last goodbye, but I would not. Nor would I go to the funeral; at the age of twelve I simply couldn't face it. Neither could I understand why they had left Granny alone in the church overnight; it seemed such a cold and heartless thing to do.

During the Park Street days, it was common practise for those in mourning to wear black armbands, and for neighbours to show sympathy by closing their curtains on the day of the funeral. Pedestrians would stop and stand silently with heads bowed as the funeral processions passed by, or the more religious amongst us might make the sign of the cross, but these small sympathetic practises seemed to die out as we left the backstreets and moved out to the suburbs.

After moving to Lillington, I found other ways of occupying my time. There were bluebell woods nearby and, in the spring, I would go there to gather armfuls of the sweet-scented flowers to take home to Mom.* Other times, I would pluck the pretty pink dog roses from the hedgerows and, in the autumn, would fill a basket with plump juicy blackberries to be made into delicious blackberry and apple pies.

Then I discovered that there was money to be made from potato picking, so at weekends and whenever there were days off school, I would make my way to the pick-up point to join the other women as they clambered aboard the tractor and trailer for a rather bumpy ride to the potato fields. There we would spread out in a long line across the field and, armed with baskets, wait for the tractor to chug past lifting the potatoes and flinging them out onto the soil ready for us to collect. One or two of the more experienced pickers might work two pitches or share a second one with a friend, whilst we youngsters usually worked one between two of us. Even then we had to be quick about it or the tractor would be turned round and on top of us again before we knew it.

At lunchtime, we would sit against the hedgerow to eat our sandwiches, and drink the tea bought to us from the farmhouse. Some of the women had babies to feed and change, whilst the others enjoyed chatting and sharing the local gossip before returning to their day's labour. At the end of it we were allowed to take home a bag of potatoes - and you can be sure that my mother furnished me with the biggest bag she had. Who could blame her when a holdall full of spuds could help to feed us for a good while.

With a limited range of foods available during those post-war years and little money coming into the house, the humble spud formed a staple part of our diet. We ate them boiled; roasted along with the Sunday joint; or cut up into chips and fried in a deep pan that never seemed to get cleaned, but simply had more lard added to it as and when needed. Other times we would enjoy the potatoes baked in the oven and still wearing their protective jackets. These took a long time to cook but were very tasty when served with a good dollop of margarine. When cooking the vegetables, Mom would boil them within an inch of their lives, but she made a delicious stew using Foster-Clarkes oxtail soup powder for flavouring, whilst her hotpot was to die for.

Puddings, when we had them, were substantial and often seemed to involve suet or milk, but sometimes we had fruit pies, baked apples or stewed plums, with the fruit often being donated by a friend who had an allotment close to our house. Mom and Horace had known each other since they were young and he would often call in on his way home from the allotment with some little treat for her. When in flower, it was sure to be Sweet Williams, as he knew she had a particular liking for these pretty little flowers.

Sometimes I would go to White Bridge with friends to swim in the river. As I had only just learned to swim, this really was not a very sensible thing to be doing but, in those early teenage years, I was oblivious to the danger I might be putting myself in. Mostly we just enjoyed ourselves splashing about in the cool, crystal-clear waters above the weir, or trying with bare hands to catch the tiny fish that darted in and out of the reeds. One year, a girl who lived nearby brought her family tent along to provide privacy when changing into our swimming costumes. What we didn't know was that a Glaswegian scout troop had just arrived for their summer camp at Offchurch Bury and they were delighted to find a group of teenage girls to annoy.

I had been to Whitebridge once before when I was much younger, this time accompanied by my sister, Rene, and her husband-to-be. Walking home again later, we passed through a field of cows. All were grazing peacefully – except for one who seemed to take a great interest in us and began following in our footsteps. As it happened, I was wearing my red blazer and, well, we all know about red rags and bulls, don't we? With the cow getting ever closer, I simply took to my heels and fled as quickly as my little legs would take me!

Sometime after we moved into the house, the Council sent out letters to their tenants telling them of a scheme to provide refrigerators to those tenants who would like them, which would be paid for by a small increase in the weekly rent. My Mother jumped at the chance and so we acquired our first fridge and began to go up in the world. Around the same time my father decided to splash out and buy a television set on hire purchase. Black and white, as all televisions were at that time, it had a minuscule screen and showed programmes for just a few hours a day. Favourites were two westerns, Rawhide and Wagon Train; and a variety show, Sunday Night at the London Palladium. This was considered by showbiz folk to be THE show to be on and if a person got top billing, then they knew they had well and truly arrived.

When a radiogram was bought to replace our old radio, Pat and I were delighted. It was a beautiful piece of furniture with a deep mirror-shine finish and was Dad's pride and joy. Now teenagers, Pat and I enjoyed listening to pop music on Radio Luxemburg, which came on air at about 6 o'clock in the evening; however, tuning in was far from easy as it could only be picked up on a very narrow wave band and would fade in and out throughout our listening. We would sit with our ears pressed up against the speakers trying to catch the words of the latest songs, but often the sound would fade away completely only to come back again in the middle of a completely different song. My favourite songster (and first teenage crush) was American singer, Pat Boone, but I seemed to be alone in my choice, since a poll held between the girls in my class at school, suggested that hip swivelling, Elvis Presley, was the runaway winner.

Mr Butler used the field behind our house to graze his cows, but it was also used by the Sports & Social club of our local Electricity Board for games of cricket and football. There was a neat pavilion at one side of the field surrounded by a white-painted picket fence enclosing a small flower garden. When the field was not being used by the cows or the sports club, we children used it as an unofficial playground and many a game of cricket or rounders took place there.

Usually these games went without incident, but during one evening game of rounders, our friend Penny tripped over one of the cricket stumps we were using to mark out the pitch, and we all looked on in horror as the pointed end went into the fleshy area of her leg just above the knee, causing globules of blood-stained fat to escape and spill out onto her skin.

By the time we moved to Lillington, Dad was working as a dustman. Unlike today, it was filthy, stinking, hard work, for which he was paid a pittance. Those were the days when dustmen were expected to collect the bins from wheresoever on the property the householder had chosen to park them. They would hoist the heavy galvanised metal bins up onto their shoulders and carry them to the dustcart waiting out on the road, then they returned them empty, back to the places from whence they came, making sure to replace lids, pick up any rubbish that may have escaped and fallen to the ground on the outward journey, and firmly closing gates behind them. Failing to do any of these could have some householders phoning or writing to complain and the men would then be reprimanded by their boss.

Dad worked an area which included Manor Farm Estate, Cloister Crofts, and Kenilworth Road, where most properties had gardens to the front and back. As the bins were usually kept at the rear of these properties, it was a heavy job made even heavier by the distance the men had to walk; How astonished Dad and his workmates would be if they could see what an easy job refuse collectors have of it today.

There was no protective clothing available for the men so they would search amongst the clothing put out as rags, hoping to find something that was still wearable. After leaving the navy and finding that factory work was too claustrophobic, my sister's husband had also become a dustman and was put to work with Dad's crew. He was adept at sorting through the discarded items and would sometimes bring home clothing for me. There was a beautiful pink satin cocktail dress that I wore to dances when I grew older; a smart royal blue suit consisting of a straight skirt and a jacket that fitted so well that it might have been made just for me; and a bikini that I wore for the first time when my husband-to-be took me to Porthcawl for the day, by way of celebrating my 18th birthday.

As a family we never had vast wardrobes of clothes and by the time I entered my teens, I hardly had any at all. Now that Pat was no longer outgrowing her clothes, not only was there nothing to be handed down to me, but there rarely seemed to be enough money to buy me any new ones. I had my school uniform, of course, which included a pretty summer dress; and there was also a grey pleated skirt with matching jacket that my mother bought from my sister's Mail Order catalogue. This was intended as a replacement for my College uniform when I started at my new school, and was worn with a pretty pale-yellow blouse purchased from Woolworth's.

I also remember a pair of bright orange jeans that had been sent to Rene by a cousin in Canada. As they were too small for her, she passed them on to me. Then one day i was wearing them when my mother sent me on an errand to the Crown Way shops. To reach them I had to walk along Mason Avenue and past the blocks of flats that were being constructed there. I was fourteen years old and barely there where womanhood was concerned, so imagine my deep embarrassment when suddenly a wolf-whistle** rang out, and I realised it was being aimed at me!

(* Note; It is now illegal to pick or uproot wild flowers, including bluebells and dog roses, but picking blackberries is still allowed as long as one obtains permission from the landowner, and the fruits are not used for commercial gain.

**Back then wolf whistles were a common way for young men to get the attention of young women, but today this could be considered sexual harassment and, if reported to the police, could possibly lead to a two-year imprisonment.)

Chapter Eighteen
Happy Days

It was something of a surprise to walk into the classroom at Clapham Terrace County Secondary School and find that half the room was taken up by boys. With the exception of the infant classes at St Peter's, all of my schooling had hitherto taken place at single-sex girls' schools, and it took a while to get used to the idea of having boys around during the school day.

Although we shared the classrooms, the two sexes were kept as far apart as was possible, with the boys sitting in rows on one side of the classroom and the girls, on the other. We had separate cloakrooms at opposite ends of the building, and separate playgrounds where a high brick wall kept us apart. We shared some lessons such as Maths and English, but were separated for PE and Games, whilst other subjects offered depended on our gender, and once a week, the whole class would head for Shrubland Street School where the boys would be taught Woodwork, whilst the girls were taught Domestic Science.

This was mainly cookery and I think we all enjoyed those lessons. At Christmas we made Christmas cakes with the lessons spread over several weeks. The first one was given over to making the cake base; the second, to making the almond paste (marzipan) and covering the base with it; and the final weeks, to making royal icing and decorating our masterpieces.

In Year Three we decorated only the tops of the cakes, spreading them with rough icing and placing tiny trees & figures to create a snow scene, but in Year Four we decorated both the top and the sides. This required us to learn two new icing techniques – flat icing and piping. First the icing was spread flat across the top of the cake until it was as smooth as the ice on an ice rink, then the sides were rough iced and the whole creation left to dry until the following week, when we would pipe a design on the tops using cone-shaped bags that we made from greaseproof paper, and fitted with metal piping nozzles of various designs. Those who didn't have the greaseproof paper to bring from home, could buy a single sheet from a corner shop opposite to the school.

Towards the end of our final year, we paired up to prepare, cook and serve a two-course meal for four, with a different pair of girls undertaking the task each week. The party of four would consist of our two selves, together with Mrs Owen, our domestic science teacher, and any other teacher of our choice - and who was brave enough to accept the invitation! It was quite a nerve-wracking experience, made the more so perhaps, since my friend and I had, rather rashly, invited a young male teacher who she had a crush on.

Another half-day per week was given over to needlework for the girls, whilst the boys worked in the school garden. Our needlework teacher, Miss Phoebe London, also taught geography and was considered to be the strictest teacher in the school, but the atmosphere was a little more relaxed during those needlework classes and we were allowed to talk quietly amongst ourselves as we worked. Like Mrs Owen, Miss London was very thorough and we always had to get each stage of our work approved before we moved on to the next.

I recall making a pair of grey-flannel pleated shorts and also a circular skirt in a yellow and white gingham fabric. There was also an embroidered table mat, a knitted cardigan and a lacy matinee jacket that I made for my sister's baby. It was Miss London who taught me how to work the lacy stitches and as I was using white wool, she advised me to encase my knitting in a clean tea towel as I worked, in order to keep it clean. This was good advice and today I always wear an apron to protect my work when using light coloured fabrics or yarns. We may not have appreciated it at the time, but we were very fortunate to have these two ladies instructing us, and I wish that I could take a step back in time and tell them so.

Both ladies had hearts of gold and when it seemed that I would not be able to sit my final year cookery exam because my mother simply couldn't afford to provide the ingredients, Mrs Owen quickly came to the rescue, providing them herself, and allowing me to make the two puddings for her. Meanwhile Miss London showed her soft side when she waylaid me as I was leaving school one evening and, taking me into her now empty classroom, quietly handed me a brown paper parcel. Opening this at home later, I found that it contained several items of clothing.

Only one half of the building was occupied by the Senior School, the other half being run as a separate Infants & Juniors. Our half mainly consisted of a large central assembly hall, which also served as a gymnasium, a dining room for those who stayed dinners; and, at times, an extra classroom. Here, also, could be found the double-door cupboard that served as the School Library and, on the opposite side of the room; the School Aquarium.

Writing in the School Magazine of 1958, two boys explain that the tank had been constructed and glazed by Fourth Year boys. They go on to say that it had been furnished with colourful rocks and interesting shells, whilst the fish included guppies and rosy barbs. I suspect that it was very much Mr Grey's baby, as he was the only teacher, I ever saw attending to it, usually accompanied by a small group of enthusiastic boys. He also kept bee-hives in the school garden and, apparently, there was a Bee Club for those who were interested. Girls were not usually allowed in the garden and I only remember visiting it once, on my very last day at the school.

A stage ran across one end of the hall, flanked on either side by large doors, one being the entrance to the girls' cloakroom and the other leading us out to the hallway that was our exit to the outside world and freedom. The space under the stage served as the headmaster's office which he shared with his secretary, Mrs Astell.

Six classrooms were arranged around the perimeter of the hall, each having glass panels set into the door, and four of them also having windows in the wall alongside, letting some natural light flow through from the classrooms. They also allowed those inside the rooms to sneak a glimpse of what was going on in the hall, although a well-aimed blackboard rubber bouncing off the wall beside a head, would very quickly remind us of where our attention should be. In truth, by the time we reached senior level we were well versed in correct classroom behaviour and there was rarely a need to reprimand. Class sizes were much bigger back then than they are today but discipline was such that we were easily controlled – and there was always the threat of the cane for those who were foolhardy enough to push their luck.

My form teacher, Mr Usher, was a rotund Mr Pickwick figure who taught English and Music. Sometimes we would be busily engaged writing an essay or parsing sentences perhaps, when we would become aware of a soft sniggering coming from the front of the class. Looking up, we would find Mr Usher sitting at his desk, shoulders shaking in merriment at some thought he had had, and which he might then proceed to share with us.

It seemed to be normal practice at that time for boys to be addressed by their Surnames and girls by their Christian names, but the young male teacher who joined the school at the beginning of Year Four, seemed unaware of this convention and took to calling the girls by their surnames too. It felt shocking; so very rude, and we couldn't have felt more astonished if he had sworn at us. Another teacher had the odd habit of walking round the class as we worked, gently tapping the top of each head with a ruler as he passed.

One day, Miss Wilde, our pretty young games teacher, asked if any of us could swim and as I had recently learned to do so, I put my hand up along with a few other girls. Shortly afterwards we were taken to Leamington Swimming Baths to demonstrate our aquatic prowess and were asked to swim two lengths of the pool freestyle. We looked at each other uncertainly, "What's that?" we whispered. Someone suggested that it meant we could use whichever stroke we chose; so off we went, some of us using breast stroke, others opting for backstroke, and the rest settling for front crawl. That we could all swim to some degree could not be questioned but it soon became very apparent that none of us were swimmers, and so any dreams Miss Wilde may have had of putting together a school swimming team was very quickly dashed.

Back in the school gym, she had us leaping over vaulting horses or struggling to climb the ropes that hung from the ceiling. Whilst some girls enjoyed this, others did not. We were going through puberty and were very aware of our changing bodies, so we were happily relieved when a new PE teacher took over and introduced us to a series of floor exercises more befitting of the young women we were becoming.

High jump took place in the boys' playground, where we were taught to do the Western Roll, with only a thick coconut mat to 'cushion' any falls. We also played netball in this playground, perhaps because it was at the far end of the school's footprint and therefore any noise was less likely to disturb those working in the classrooms. I was somewhat surprised to find myself appointed reserve for the netball team. As I have previously explained, my enthusiasm for sports far outweighed my ability, so I can only think that it was a case of me being the best of the rest At any rate, I never did get to play and my main role seemed to be setting out the after-match orange squash and biscuits, along with the opposing team's reserve.

When Mom could afford it, I would have school dinners; when she could not, I would take sandwiches. At the beginning of the week these might consist of two decently-thick slices of bread joined together by a slice of luncheon meat, but as the week progressed the slices would get thinner and thinner, with dainty slivers of cucumber or a thin spread of fish paste providing the filling; however, by Friday, there was often nothing more than margarine scrapped from the wrapper, to hold the two slices together. With no money left in her purse, it was the best she could do until my father received his weekly pay packet and I suspect that she often went hungry herself.

Each Fourth-Year pupil took a turn at reading out the Lesson in morning assembly. Following on from those elocution lessons at the Girls' College, I was acutely aware of the sound of my voice and so, perhaps, even more nervous than I might otherwise have been, as I stood alone on the stage with so many pairs of eyes staring up at me. Keeping my own eyes firmly fixed on the pages of the Bible as I read, I fought to control the nerves that seemed determined not to be controlled, almost collapsing with relief when my ordeal was finally over.

It was during my first year at the school that I suffered my first attack of migraine and it was a very frightening experience. We were in morning assembly singing from our hymn books when the first symptoms appeared. I loved singing hymns and was happily in full throttle when, glancing down at my book, I was alarmed to discover that I could only see a small part of the page. I know now that such visual disturbances are part and parcel of classic migraine but, unfamiliar with the condition back then, I thought that I must be going blind. Incredibly, frightened as I was, I didn't tell anyone what was happening. I just didn't dare. With the ear thing still very fresh in my mind, I was too afraid of my mother's reaction to take the risk of her getting to know, and I just kept it to myself.

As he was our music teacher, Mr Usher was in charge of preparing us for the annual Christmas Carol Concert. This was when I first encountered the gentle Coventry Carol, and also learned that The Holly and the Ivy actually had more than one verse to it. One year I found myself in the front row of the choir, standing directly opposite to the mayor. As we sang, I noticed his eyes slowly close but only when his wife suddenly gave him a sharp elbow in the ribs, did it become obvious that the poor man had actually fallen asleep!

It was during this concert that our Christmas cakes were put on display in one of the classrooms. Since they were being safely stored away at Shrubland Street School where we had our cookery lessons, we had to collect them at lunchtime on the day and convey them by foot to Clapham Terrace. Usually when making our way between the two buildings we would take the short cut over the ladder bridge that crossed the canal, but in order to minimise the risk of accidents, on this occasion we were instructed to take the longer route, and to be careful not to jolt our boxes in case the fragile piping should break.

Back in the classroom, we were relieved to find that all of the cakes had survived the journey intact and for the next while we proudly sat guarding them against inquisitive boys whilst we awaited further instructions. After some time had passed, I was called out with some other girls to help construct a makeshift display stand in one of the other rooms. Imagine my dismay then, when, upon returning to my own classroom, I discovered that my cake had been sabotaged in my absence and part of the delicate piping now lay in pieces across the top. There was little that could be done about it other than to manoeuvre the broken pieces back into position with a knife and then hide the cake away at the back of the display where it was hoped that no-one would notice.

During the summer Open Evening, a makeshift catwalk was erected down the centre of the hall for the girls to model the garments they had made, and when that was cleared away the boys would take over and give an impressive PE display. They would also have the opportunity to show their parents around the school garden.

Meanwhile, other work was displayed in the classrooms where parents could mingle and chat with the teachers if they so desired.

My parents never came to any of the events at any of the schools I attended. I didn't really expect my father to come, for he was of his day and regarded anything to do with his children as my mother's responsibility, whilst she would simply reply to my pleading with an impatient," Oh, I'll 'ave t' see if I've got the time". But she never did, and it was always a great disappointment when I had worked so hard at something, and no one turned up to see me perform or to admire the work put on display.

Mr Usher seemed to have a penchant for Scottish folk songs and if we were not busy learning the words to all of those Christmas Carols, then he might well have us visiting the Bonnie, Bonnie Banks of Loch Lomond or, perhaps, accompanying Bonnie Prince Charlie as he travelled over the Sea to Skye.

During English lessons, we visited Hiawatha, The Lady of Shallot and The Ancient Mariner. We also became acquainted with Shakespeare and I recollect going to Stratford to see one of the Shakespeare plays at The Shakespeare Memorial Theatre. As the school didn't have its own transport, we travelled by bus. This was long before the stretch of road between Warwick and Stratford was besmirched by the complicated road system that is known today as Longbridge Island, and for those of us who rarely ventured beyond the confines of our Spa town, just travelling through the beautiful Warwickshire countryside was a treat in itself.

English was one of my favourite subjects and I particularly loved writing compositions; however, I was less keen to tackle parsing exercises and would struggle with these even today. Corrected spelling mistakes had to be written out three times at the bottom of each essay, and Mr Usher would not accept the words 'have got' declaring that if you **have** something then you've already **got** it. Surely the poor man must be constantly turning in his grave today, every time someone announces '**I was sat**' or '**I was stood**'. As for '**gonna**', '**gunna**' and '**jography**'…

I have in my possession a school copy book dating back to 1912, which belonged to my husband's aunt. One of twelve children, she was born and raised on her parent's small farm in southern Ireland, where she attended a tiny country school which served the needs of the children from all the farms around and about. You might suppose that they received a simple elementary education, but you would be wrong, for as Aunt Bridge's book shows, even a hundred plus years ago the children of Ireland were busy parsing their sentences, writing business letters and compiling compositions on subjects as diverse as The Skin and The Pencil.

Some people of my generation, consider themselves hard done by because they didn't get into Grammar School. They claim that Secondary School meant a second-rate education and prevented them from achieving their maximum potential in life. For some people, this may have been so, but I have no complaints about my own secondary education and I know that a number of my fellow pupils went on to get degrees and/or professional qualifications.

Chapter Nineteen
The End of Childhood

The headmaster, Mr Grey, was not long at the school himself but had already made a number of changes, one of the first being to introduce a uniform. A simple arrangement consisting of grey trousers and white shirts for the boys, and grey skirts with yellow blouses for the girls. There was also a yellow and black striped tie, and a black blazer for all. At the time of its introduction, it was compulsory for all the new Year One intake but was optional for the older children already at the school. Although a very simple and inexpensive outfit, it did look extremely smart.

He also introduced a School Magazine * which makes for very interesting reading – more so from this distance perhaps, than it did even at the time it was printed. There had been three magazines published by the time I left the school and I had essays in both the second and the third of these, which covered the two years I was there, whilst my cousin, Pat Owen, had poems published in all three.

On my first morning, I stood uncertainly at the front of the class until Mr Usher directed me towards the only vacant seat. The girl occupying the other half of the desk beamed with pleasure as I made my way towards her and was very obviously delighted to be having a companion. Her name was Frances O'Donnell and we soon became good friends. Her father was in the RAF and the family lived in married quarters at RAF Gaydon, which made out-of-school socialising difficult, but I did borrow my sister's bike one time and cycle out to visit her.

We were of an age when boys suddenly seemed to look more interesting, and wet playtimes might well have found us sitting on the radiators in the hall, giggling over whichever boys were currently taking our fancy. The Fourth-Year pupils were allowed to stay in their classrooms during breaks, where the girls would often take out their knitting or sewing, whilst the boys... What did they do? Memory says that they simply gathered around a certain bunch of girls to talk and tease.

At that time, we left school at the end of the term in which we turned fifteen. This, then, might explain why I suddenly found myself elevated to the position of Prefect for my last trimester at the school. I was certainly not Prefect material, but with others leaving at the end of each term, they had little choice but to replace them from an ever-dwindling list of candidates.

At the end of Clapham Terrace, a zebra crossing spanned the width of Radford Road, put there, no doubt, to help we school children cross in safety. Quite often this would be controlled by WPC Gladys Pemberton who was not a woman to be messed about.

Seeing my friend on the opposite side of the road one day, I waited impatiently for Gladys to give the signal to cross and then, when she did so, I started to run, only to be stopped in my tracks by the sound of her voice. She proceeded to give me a very public telling off for running, and then sent me back to the beginning to do the walk of shame. It was deeply embarrassing, not least because, as a prefect, I was expected to show a good example to the other pupils.

It was Christmas 1957 and, being the last one before we left the school, it was decided that the fourth-Year party would be a more grown-up affair with ballroom dancing and jiving; however, that didn't stop the teachers from introducing some party games and, after a while, we were instructed to form ourselves into two lines each consisting of boy/girl, boy/girl.

Frances had a crush on a boy we will call A, and managed to squeeze herself in between him and his friend B, whilst I, having a crush on that young man, tucked myself in behind him. It was then that the teachers revealed the object of the game was to pass an orange down the line from under our chins and with hands clasped firmly behind our backs.

Well, it is one thing to drool over the object of your juvenile desire when separated by several desks, quite another to suddenly find yourself in such close and intimate contact with him. Such was my embarrassment that when I met B again many, many years later, memories of the party instantly came flooding back and I could barely bring myself to speak to him.

An even greater source of embarrassment came at my final school medical when, to my horror, I discovered that SHE was now a HE... and that, clad only in my navy school knickers, I was expected to parade in front of him whilst he studied me closely for any abnormalities. Even worse, without so much as a by-your-leave, he suddenly gripped the waist band of my pants and peered down at THAT! And then he demanded that I cough so that he could get an even better look!

Another toe-curling moment came when I was chosen to model in profile for the art class. At the age of thirteen and going through puberty, it wasn't only the shape of my body that was changing and my father, rather cruelly, had taken to teasing me about the size of my nose. Like most young girls, I was very conscious of my looks and perhaps my father's teasing made me even more so than most. At any rate, I felt absolutely mortified as I quietly sat there whilst the rest of the class studied my 'parrot beak' in minute detail. Why on earth did Mr Johnson choose me? Why not one of the prettier girls? Or one of the boys?

There was no harm intended in my father's teasing. He was what he was, the product of his own neglectful upbringing, and simply would not have considered the negative effects his teasing might be having on his daughter. Indeed, so neglectful were his own parents that they were imprisoned for child neglect and each sentenced to several months of hard labour. Two of their sons were put into the care of the Middlemore Children's Home in Birmingham, before being taken across the Atlantic to New Brunswick in Canada, where they were housed with local farming families.

By the time the new school year began in September 1957, Mr Johnson had temporarily jumped ship to the USA and was working at a school in Huntington, Indiana. In his place now was a young American woman who normally worked in the Huntington school. With her distinctive American style of dress, the sneakers, and the hair arranged in a French Roll at the back of her head, she looked very different to the other women teachers and soon became immensely popular.

Writing in the school magazine before heading back to The States, she tells how surprised she had been when arriving in England for the first time, "to see the grass of a vivid green I had always associated only with golf courses, stretching as far as the eye could see." A sentiment echoed by my husband's niece and her family (who also live in the USA) when they visited England for the first time, in 2014.

Miss Oyer concludes that "England feels like home and I will be back many times before I finally settle down to be an old woman." Well, I can't say if she ever did come back, but she certainly lived to be an old woman, for she died as recently as October 2015, at the grand old age of 95.

The careers people sat behind a table on the curtained-off stage and called us up for interview one by one. I had expected that they would chat to me, find out about my academic strengths and weaknesses, my hobbies and interests, and then suggest areas of employment that they thought might appeal. But no. They simply asked if I had any idea what I would like to do. Since I had very limited knowledge of the range of jobs that might be available out there, the true answer to that would have been a blunt

"No", but instead I found myself suggesting that I might like to work in a florist perhaps, or a bakery, where I could be trained to decorate cakes. This was noted and then I was dismissed.

A few days later I received a letter informing me that although they hadn't been able to find work for me at a florist, they had been able to arrange an interview with Mr Chesterfield at Elizabeth the Chef. I dressed carefully in the smart blue suit that my brother-in-law had rescued from a dustbin, and made my way nervously to their offices above the shop on The Parade. Heart pounding with nerves, I climbed the steep narrow staircase and knocked at a door. A woman's voice bade me "come in" and, opening the door I found myself in a small room furnished with a desk, behind which sat a middle-aged woman. She looked at me enquiringly and I explained my business. "Oh yes. Well, I'm afraid Mr Chesterfield had to go out so he won't be able to see you after all," she said, and then went back to her typing.

In fact, although I love flowers, as my idea of flower arranging is usually limited to simply plonking a bunch straight into a vase, I couldn't have been more unsuited to that particular job. As for Elizabeth the Chef; Their loss!!!

The careers people offered no further help and so I was on my own. Every day I scoured the Jobs Vacant section of The Morning News but it wasn't until the week I was leaving school that I saw something suitable; The International Stores were looking for an assistant, no experience necessary.

When I arrived home from school on Thursday afternoon, my mother told me that the shop manager had called to see me. She had invited him in and immediately he had spotted my sister's wedding photo. Rene had worked at the shop for a short time before leaving to have her first child and Mr Porter had recognised her instantly. It was enough. If I was anything like my sister, he declared, then he would be happy to offer me a job. After school the next day I called to see him as requested, and he must have liked what he saw because he told me I could start work on Monday morning, at 8.30 sharp. Childhood was behind me and I was about to enter the adult world.

(*My thanks go to Richard Fisk for the loan of his copies of the Clapham Terrace school magazines. They were much appreciated.)

APPENDIX 1

My Paternal Grandparents

My mother had a tendency to exaggerate. Or she might simply muddle her facts, so when she mentioned one day that my father's parents had been imprisoned for child neglect, I took little notice simply thinking that she had become confused by the village tittle-tattle passed on to her over the years.

Not until my son started to explore the family tree some years later, did we discover that her accusation was, in fact, true - and more shocking than we might ever have visioned.

A visit to Warwick Records Office revealed that In October 1907, William Cleaver of Cubbington and his wife, Frances, were summoned for wilfully and unlawfully neglecting their children in a manner likely to cause them unnecessary suffering or injury to their health. The children were Albert 14, Charles 11, Henry 7, Frederick 5, Cyril 4, and John Henry 6 months. Both pleaded not guilty.

Giving evidence to the court, Charles Nye, Inspector for the NSPCC, testified that on October 10th he had visited the village school with PS Butcher and Doctor Hicks, where they found three of the children – Charles, Henry, and Frederick. They were in a grossly neglected state, filthily dirty, ill clad, bodies covered in sores and vermin. Their shirts were little more than rags and covered in vermin marks. They looked ill-nourished, pale and puny.

Dr Hicks stated that he saw Charles and Henry at the school. They were miserably clad and Charles' shirt was so ragged that it was tumbling to pieces. He was the worst of the two with his body covered in eczema. He was anaemic, of a leaden colour and badly nourished.

The men then visited the defendants' house where they found the other three children, including Albert who was in a similar state of poor nutrition, covered with vermin marks and ill-clad. He had been in the hospital but the doctor did not know if that was from this bad state or whether the state of nutrition was caused by the illness. The baby was not so bad.

The bedrooms were in a filthy and shocking state; they contained no washing arrangements; the mattresses were in a sodden and verminous condition and there were no blankets. The state of the home and children was the result of long and continued neglect and had undoubtably affected the health of the children. This was not poverty because that is easily distinguishable from neglect.

Inspector Nye said that he had visited the house on August 1st and from what he saw, he had occasion to warn the defendants, stating that "One of the boys was in a horrible condition at that time and I had to get to the other side of the room, the stench was so great." He asked the boy if he ever had a bath, and he replied that he couldn't ever recollect having one.

Major Gibson asked, "Is the woman able to do her work? She does not appear to be in good health." To which the doctor replied that it was the filthy conditions of the house and she is suffering in a similar way to the children.

The village schoolmaster, Mr Robotham, gave similar evidence adding that in the matter of scholarship, the boys had not been able to keep up with the other children and he had had lots of complaints from parents because of their children sitting together. In July, they were in such a state that he had to send them home, partly because he could see that Albert was visibly dwindling away. He was sent to the hospital where he stayed a long time.

Superintendent Ravenhall stated that William Cleaver had been convicted at that very court on four occasions for using obscene language and his wife had been convicted at Leamington for being drunk in charge of a child. PS Butcher added that the husband was more or less drunk on Saturday nights and all day on Sunday.

After retiring to consider the case, the magistrates found both defendants guilty, saying that they found the case to be the worst they had ever heard and sentencing both parents to four months in prison with hard labour, whilst the children would go to the workhouse where they would be carefully looked after.

In fact, they would almost certainly have been sent to one of the Warwick Union Children's Homes in Leamington, where they would have been bathed and had their heads shaved to rid them of the lice, before being put into a decent set of clothes.

I was shocked by what I read. Cubbington was a small village and all the evidence suggested that the family was well known to the various authorities, so how on earth had the children been allowed to get into such a state before anyone Intervened?

APPENDIX 2

Albert & Charles Cleaver

In January 1908 Mr George Nye, Inspector for the NSPCC, made an application for custody of Albert Cleaver (14) and Charles Cleaver (11) to be transferred from their parents, William and Frances Cleaver, who were convicted on October 16th for child neglect, to the care of Mr. George Jackson, Secretary of the Middlemore Homes, Birmingham. This was granted.

A report in the Middlemore Application Book dated June 23rd 1908, states that the parents were very quarrelsome with each other, a divided household & children badly neglected in consequence...The children were a mass of filth and covered with eczema from dirt. Bedding was in a most rotten condition from urine and excreta and had to be all burned & the children were in a very emaciated condition.

Both boys were sent to Canada, sailing on The Carthaginian from Liverpool on 16th May 1908, and arriving in Halifax, Nova Scotia on 28th May. They were part of a group of children travelling together. From Halifax they travelled on to New Brunswick where Albert was settled with Mr John McBean Senior. Farmer, of Taymouth, York,

New Brunswick, whilst Charles was settled with Mr James S Young, also a farmer of Taymouth, York, New Brunswick.

The boys were visited once a year by a Middlemore inspector until they reached the age of 18. They were always said to be in good health and to have a sufficient supply of clothing; they had no complaints; the homes were satisfactory and they attended Church and Sunday School regularly.

The Inspector's remarks for Charles are as follows:

1909: Boy seems very small for his age and I should say that a mistake has been made – looks about ten years old. Mr and Mrs Young are well pleased with him and boy is perfectly happy.

1910: Very small boy for age.

1913:Mrs Young says boy will soon be hiking (possibly living) out on his own account now. Boy grown some but still rather small for his age.

1914: Charles is going to work on Valley Rail Road and will earn 0.80 a day & board. He has been a good boy whilst with the Youngs and he can make his home with them whenever he wants to. He will help them with work at cropping time and get Board & L whenever he wants it. Gets $10 a year for cleaning (possibly 'clothing`) & lunch.

<u>However, the Inspector's remarks for Albert are rather less positive.</u>

<u>1909</u>: Not too fond of work and won't go to school. Albert does not get along with the women folk in the house. I had a talk with Albert and he has promised to do better.

<u>1910</u>: Small boy for his age, Goes to school in the winter.

<u>1911</u>: Boy is really not worth wages. Very slow to grasp things and I rather think that he is somewhat mentally weak.

<u>1912</u>: Boy is somewhat feeble minded & it is well if he can remain where he is at no wages, as it would be hard to resettle him. He is said to be untruthful.

(Although the Inspectors question the boys ages, they are correct.)

We believe that Charles died on June 25th 1967 from a CVA and Bronchopneumonia. He appears to have continued living with the Youngs who are described as his foster parents on the death certificate we have. (Another source states that he was the adopted child of the Youngs.)

Unfortunately, we have no more information on Albert at this time but it is interesting to note that the McBeans seem never to have asked for him to be removed in spite of the problems they appear to have had with him.

APPENDIX 3

Do not criticise your neighbour until you have walked a mile in his moccasins

It would be easy to sit here in the comfort of my own home and label my grandparents as cruel and uncaring, but I did not live their lives. I do not know what stresses and strains they may have lived through that led them to be so neglectful of their children, and without all of the facts it would be unfair to judge them.

My grandmother's death certificate states that she died from coma, diabetes, gangrene of the toes and old age. (She was 82 when she died on the 31st July 1942).

My grandfather's death certificate indicates that he had also been very ill in the years before his death on 21st January 1933, with causes of death stated to be Influenza and congestion of the lungs; bronchitis and emphysema.

During their trial, one of the magistrates commented "Is the woman able to do her work? She does not appear to be in good health." To which Dr Hicks replied that it was the filthy condition of the house and she was suffering in similar ways to the children.

Could not the doctor have been wrong? Even at the time of the trial, could she not have been suffering the effects of the diabetes, and simply unable to care for the children?

The schoolmaster, Mr Robotham, stated that he had known the family for a considerable time and whilst the first three children* were in a satisfactory condition, the last four came to school neglected and dirty, and apparently very ill-nourished. This suggests that she had not always been so neglectful, so why the change?

My grandfather worked at the woodyard in Milverton. This would have been a dusty environment and might account for his emphysema. Little was known about emphysema and diabetes at the start of the twentieth century and bearing in mind that the NHS was not formed until 1948, the family may not have had the means to seek medical assistance, even if treatment had been available.

I am not making excuses for my grandparents, but simply pointing out that we should not be too quick to judge. From the evidence given at the trial, it is clear that the family were well known to the various authorities, yet none of them seem to have stepped in to help until one of the boys appears to have been at death's door, so were they not also guilty of neglect?

And when he was asked about my grandmother's health during the trial, the doctor's reply seems to have been quite dismissive. Had he examined her before reaching his conclusion? There is nothing in the court reports to indicate that he had done so.

Were they really the cruel parents the court case suggests? We need to remember that they lived in a time when just existing was exhausting work for the poverty classes. Can any of us be sure that we would have coped any better given their circumstances?

(*The three older children mentioned by the schoolmaster, had already left the school by the time of the trial.)

Printed in Great Britain
by Amazon